FIGHTING
TERRORISM

How Democracies Can Defeat
the International Terrorist Network

FIGHTING TERRORISM

How Democracies Can Defeat
the International Terrorist Network

2001 EDITION

BENJAMIN
NETANYAHU

FARRAR, STRAUS AND GIROUX

New York

Farrar, Straus and Giroux
19 Union Square West, New York 10003

LIBRARY OF CONGRESS CATALOGING-IN-PUBLICATION DATA
Netanyahu, Binyamin.
    Fighting terrorism: how democracies can defeat the
international terrorist network / Benjamin Netanyahu.
        p. cm.
    Includes bibliographical references and index.
    ISBN 0-374-15492-9 (alk. paper)
    1. Terrorism.   2. Terrorism—Prevention—Government policy.
I. Title.
HV6431.N48   1995
363.3'2—dc20   95–4849

Paperback ISBN: 0-374-52497-1

10 9 8 7 6 5 4

To all the victims of terror,
and to the sons and daughters of liberty
who will defeat the evil that struck down their brethren,
and so save our world

ACKNOWLEDGMENTS

My first vote of thanks must go to Dr. Yoram Hazony of the Shalem Center–National Policy Institute in Jerusalem, who, not for the first time, shouldered the burden of being my editor, my research director, and my all-around sounding board. It was with him that I discussed and tested all the ideas in this book, drawing especially on his expertise in political philosophy to sharpen and hone the legal and moral aspects of a democracy's response to the dilemma of fighting terrorism while preserving civil liberties.

Colonel (res.) Yigal Carmon, a former adviser on terrorism to two Israeli prime ministers, deserves my heartfelt thanks for unstintingly making available to me his unique obervations on the operational methods of fighting terrorism. In this he drew not only from his own rich professional experience in Israel but also from his insights gleaned from a vast network of contacts with anti-terror authorities in many lands, examples of which I have used liberally throughout these pages.

I am grateful to Boaz Ganor, a specialist on terrorism at the Hebrew University in Jerusalem, for having read the entire manuscript, offering important comments which served to clarify and amplify many passages.

I am much indebted to my publisher, Roger Straus, who with his boundless élan and unmatched nerve prodded me to write this book while in the throes of Israel's less than genteel politics. Roger's encouragement on the need to clearly state the fundamentals of fighting terrorism in the 1990s were as valuable to me as they were during our earlier collaboration on this subject in the 1980s. The form of the problem has changed, the need to address it has not.

My colleague and friend Ron Dermer has lately served as a much-valued intellectual gadfly. In the days following the terror bombings in America, his keen and critical intelligence helped focus my thoughts on the concepts necessary to wage battle against a resurgent terror at the beginning of a new century.

I owe my deepest appreciation to my wife, Sara. Her clear mind and compassionate heart helped see me through many difficult days. By reminding me always that behind the unfathomable numbers of terrorism's victims lie the ruins of broken lives and shattered hopes, she renewed a decades-old conviction that I must do all in my power to help win the war against this unmitigated evil. That is what each of us is now asked to do.

CONTENTS

ix

Foreword to the
2001 Edition

September 11, 2001, was a day that future historians will call a hinge of history. On that day, a lethal blow was struck in the heart of freedom. From that day on, international terrorism could no longer be considered a tactical threat with no real global implications. On that morning, it became apparent that a terrible and perfidious force was endangering the free world.

The first edition of this book, published in 1995, described this danger—its genesis, its growth, its ambitions, and the terrible consequences to our world if it was not immediately addressed. This danger is now apparent to all but the most obtuse.

What I have to add to the first edition is summarized in the following remarks, which I made in the United States Congress on September 20, little more than a week after the terror bombings in New York and Washington. Although these remarks include some material developed in the book, they are printed here in their entirety as a foreword to this edition, for I believe that they represent the principles and basic conceptions that must guide our actions in the great and crucial war that lies ahead.

What is at stake today is nothing less than the survival of our civilization. There may be some who would have thought ten days ago that to talk in these apocalyptic terms about the battle against international terrorism was to engage in reckless exaggeration. No longer.

Each one of us today understands that we are all targets, that our cities are vulnerable, and that our values are hated with an unmatched fanaticism that seeks to destroy our societies and our way of life.

I am certain that I speak on behalf of my entire nation when I say: *Today, we are all Americans.* In grief, as in defiance. In grief, because my people have faced the agonizing horrors of terror for many decades, and we feel an instant kinship both with the victims of this tragedy and with the great nation that mourns its fallen brothers and sisters. In defiance, because just as my country continues to fight terrorism in our battle for survival, I know that America will not cower before this challenge.

I have absolute confidence that if we, the citizens of the free world, led by President Bush, marshal the enormous reserves of power at our disposal, harness the steely resolve of a free people, and mobilize our collective will, we shall eradicate this evil from the face of the earth.

But to achieve this goal, we must first answer several questions: Who are the evil forces responsible for this terrorist onslaught? What is their motive? And most important, what must be done to defeat them?

The first and most crucial thing to understand is this: There is *no* international terrorism without the support of sovereign states. International terrorism simply cannot be sustained for long without the regimes that aid and abet it. Terrorists are not suspended in midair. They train, arm, and indoctrinate their killers from within safe havens on territory provided by terrorist states. Often these regimes provide the terrorists with intelligence, money, and operational assistance, dispatching them to serve as deadly proxies to wage a hidden war against more powerful enemies.

These regimes mount a worldwide propaganda campaign to legitimize terror, besmirching its victims and exculpating its practitioners—as we witnessed in the farcical spectacle of the UN conference on racism in Durban last month. Iran, Libya, and Syria call the United States and Israel racist countries that abuse human rights? Even Orwell could not have imagined such a world.

Take away all this state support, and the entire scaffolding of international terrorism will collapse into dust.

The international terrorist network is thus based on regimes—Iran, Iraq, Syria, Taliban Afghanistan, Yasir

Arafat's Palestinian Authority, and several other Arab regimes, such as the Sudan. These regimes are the ones that harbor the terrorist groups: Osama bin Laden in Afghanistan; Hizballah and others in Syrian-controlled Lebanon; Hamas, Islamic Jihad, and the recently mobilized Fatah and Tanzim factions in the Palestinian territories; and sundry other terror organizations based in such capitals as Damascus, Baghdad, and Khartoum.

These terrorist states and terror organizations together form a *terror network* whose constituent parts support one another operationally as well as politically. For example, the Palestinian groups cooperate closely with Hizballah, which in turn links them to Syria, Iran, and bin Laden. These offshoots of terror have affiliates in other states that have not yet uprooted their presence, such as Egypt, Yemen, and Saudi Arabia.

The growth of this terror network is the result of several developments in the last two decades. Chief among them is the Khomeini revolution and the establishment of a clerical Islamic state in Iran. This created a sovereign spiritual base for fomenting a strident Islamic militancy worldwide—a militancy that was often backed by terror.

Equally important was the victory in the Afghan war of the international *Mujahdeen* brotherhood. This international band of zealots, whose ranks include Osama bin Laden, saw their victory over the Soviet Union as providential proof of the innate supremacy of faithful Moslems over the weak infidel powers. They believed that even the superior weapons of a superpower could not withstand their superior will.

To this should be added Saddam Hussein's escape from destruction at the end of the Gulf War, his dismissal of UN monitors, and his growing confidence that he can soon develop unconventional weapons to match those of the West.

Finally, the creation of Yasir Arafat's terror enclave gave a safe haven to militant Islamic terrorist groups such as Hamas and Islamic Jihad. Like their *Mujahdeen* cousins, they drew inspiration from Israel's hasty withdrawal from Lebanon, glorified as a great Moslem victory by the Syrian-backed Hizballah. Under Arafat's rule, these Palestinian Islamic terrorist groups have made repeated use of the technique of suicide bombing, going so far as to run summer camps in Gaza that teach Palestinian children how to become suicide martyrs.

Here is what Arafat's government-controlled newspaper, *Al-Hayat-Al-Jadida*, said on September 11, a few hours before the suicide bombings of the World Trade Center and the Pentagon: "The suicide bombers of today are the noble successors of the Lebanese suicide bombers, who taught the U.S. Marines a tough lesson in [Lebanon] . . . These suicide bombers are the salt of the earth, the engines of history . . . They are the most honorable people among us."

A simple rule prevails here: The success of terrorists in one part of the terror network emboldens terrorists throughout the network.

This then is the Who. Now for the Why.

Although its separate parts may have local objectives and take part in local conflicts, the main motivation driving the terror network is an anti-Western hostility that seeks to achieve nothing less than a reversal of history. It seeks to roll back the West and install an extremist form of Islam as the dominant power in the world. And it seeks to do this not by means of its own advancement and progress, but by destroying the enemy. This hatred is the product of a seething resentment that has simmered for centuries in certain parts of the Arab and Islamic world.

Most Moslems in the world, including the vast majority of the growing Moslem communities in the West, are not guided by this interpretation of history, nor are they moved by its call for a holy war against the West. But some are. And though their numbers are small compared to the peaceable majority, they nevertheless constitute a growing hinterland for this militancy.

Militant Islamists resented the West for pushing back the triumphant march of Islam into the heart of Europe many centuries ago. Believing in the innate supremacy of Islam, they then suffered a series of shocks when in the last two centuries that same hated, supposedly inferior West penetrated Islamic realms in North Africa, the Middle East, and the Persian Gulf.

For them the mission was clear: The West had to be pushed out of these areas. Pro-Western Middle Eastern regimes were toppled in rapid succession, including in

Iran. And Israel, the Middle East's only democracy and its purest manifestation of Western progress and freedom, must be wiped off the face of the earth.

Thus, *the soldiers of militant Islam do not hate the West because of Israel, they hate Israel because of the West*—because they see it is an island of Western democratic values in a Moslem-Arab sea of despotism. That is why they call Israel the Little Satan, to distinguish it clearly from the country that has always been and will always be the Great Satan—the United States of America.

Nothing better illustrates this than Osama bin Laden's call for a *jihad*, or holy war, against the United States in 1998. He gave as his primary reason not Israel, not the Palestinians, not the "peace process," but rather the very presence of the United States "occupying the Land of Islam in the holiest of places." And where is that? The Arabian peninsula, says bin Laden, where America is "plundering its riches, dictating to its rulers, and humiliating its people." Israel, by the way, comes a distant third, after "the continuing aggression against the Iraqi people" (*Al-Quds-Al-Arabi*, February 23, 1998). For the bin Ladens of the world, Israel is merely a sideshow. America is the target.

But reestablishing a resurgent Islam requires not just rolling back the West; it requires destroying its main engine, the United States. And if the United States cannot be destroyed just now, it first can be humiliated—as in the Teheran hostage crisis two decades ago—and then ferociously attacked again and again, until it is brought to its knees. But the ultimate goal remains the same: Destroy America and win eternity.

Some may find it hard to believe that Islamic militants truly cling to the mad fantasy of destroying America. There should be no mistake about it. They do. And unless they are stopped now, their attacks will continue, and will become even more lethal in the future.

To understand the true dangers of Islamic militancy, we can compare it to another ideology which sought world domination—communism. Both movements pursued irrational goals, but the communists at least pursued theirs in a rational way. Any time they had to choose between ideology and their own survival, as in Cuba or Berlin, they backed off and chose survival. Not so for the Islamic militants. They pursue an irrational ideology *irrationally*—with no apparent regard for human life, neither their own lives nor the lives of their enemies. The communists seldom, if ever, produced suicide bombers, while Islamic militancy produces hordes of them, glorifying them and promising them that their dastardly deeds will earn them a luxurious afterlife. This highly pathological aspect of Islamic militancy is what makes it so deadly for mankind.

In 1995, when I wrote *Fighting Terrorism*, I warned about the militant Islamic groups operating in the West with the support of foreign powers—serving as a new breed of "domestic-international" terrorists, basing themselves in America to wage *jihad* against America:

"Such groups," I wrote then, "nullify in large measure

the need to have air power or intercontinental missiles as delivery systems for an Islamic nuclear payload. *They* will be the delivery system. In the worst of such scenarios, the consequence could be not a car bomb but a *nuclear* bomb in the basement of the World Trade Center."

Well, they did not use a nuclear bomb. They used two 150-ton fully fueled jetliners to wipe out the Twin Towers. But does anyone doubt that, given the chance, they will throw atom bombs at America and its allies? And perhaps, long before that, chemical and biological weapons?

This is the greatest danger facing our common future. Some states of the terror network already possess chemical and biological capabilities, and some are feverishly developing nuclear weapons. Can one rule out the possibility that they will be tempted to use such weapons, openly or through terror proxies, or that their weapons might fall into the hands of the terrorist groups they harbor?

We have received a wake-up call from hell. Now the question is simple: Do we rally to defeat this evil, while there is still time, or do we press a collective snooze button and go back to business as usual?

The time for action is now.

Today the terrorists have the will to destroy us, but they do not have the power. There is no doubt that we have the power to crush them. Now we must also show that we have the will. Once any part of the terror network acquires nuclear weapons, this equation will fundamentally change—and with it the course of human affairs. This is the historical imperative that now confronts us all.

And now the third question: What do we about it? First, as President Bush said, we must make no distinction between the terrorists and the states that support them. It is not enough to root out the terrorists who committed this horrific act of war. We must dismantle the entire terrorist network.

If any part of it remains intact, it will rebuild itself, and the specter of terrorism will reemerge and strike again. Bin Laden, for example, has shuttled over the last decade from Saudi Arabia to Afghanistan to the Sudan and back again. So we must not leave any base intact.

To achieve this goal we must first have moral clarity. We must fight terror wherever and whenever it appears. We must make all states play by the same rules. We must declare terrorism a crime against humanity, and we must consider the terrorists enemies of mankind, to be given no quarter and no consideration for their purported grievances. If we begin to distinguish between acts of terror, justifying some and repudiating others based on sympathy with this or that cause, we will lose the moral clarity that is so essential for victory.

This clarity is what enabled America and Britain to root out piracy in the nineteenth century. This same clarity enabled the Allies to root out Nazism in the twentieth century. They did not look for the "root cause" of piracy or the "root cause" of Nazism—because they knew that some acts are evil in and of themselves, and do not deserve any consideration or "understanding." They did not ask whether Hitler was right about the alleged wrong done to Germany at Versailles. That they left to the historians. The leaders of the Western Alliance said something else: Nothing justifies Nazism. Nothing!

We must be equally clear-cut today: Nothing justifies terrorism. Nothing!

Terrorism is defined neither by the identity of its perpetrators nor by the cause they espouse. Rather, it is defined by the nature of the act. Terrorism is the deliberate attack on innocent civilians. In this it must be distinguished from legitimate acts of war that target combatants and may unintentionally harm civilians.

When the British bombed the Copenhagen Gestapo headquarters in 1944 and one of their bombs unintentionally struck a children's hospital, that was a tragedy, but it was not terrorism. When a few weeks ago Israel fired a missile that killed two Hamas arch-terrorists and two Palestinian children who were playing nearby were tragically struck down, that was not terrorism.

Terrorists do not *unintentionally* harm civilians. They *deliberately* murder, maim, and menace civilians—as many as possible.

No cause, no grievance, no apology can ever justify terrorism. Terrorism against Americans, Israelis, Spaniards, Britons, Russians, or anyone else is all part of the same evil and must be treated as such. It is time to establish a fixed principle for the international community: Any cause that uses terrorism to advance its aims will not be rewarded. On the contrary, it will be punished and placed beyond the pale.

Armed with this moral clarity in *defining* terrorism, we must possess an equal moral clarity in *fighting* it. If we include Iran, Syria, and the Palestinian Authority in the coalition to fight terror—even though they currently harbor, sponsor, and dispatch terrorists—then the alliance against terror will be defeated from within.

Perhaps we may achieve a short-term objective of destroying one terrorist fiefdom, but this will preclude the possibility of overall victory. Such a coalition will melt down because of its own internal contradictions. We might win a battle. We will certainly lose the war.

These regimes, like all terrorist states, must be given a forthright demand: Stop terrorism, permanently, or you will face the wrath of the free world—through harsh and sustained political, economic, and military sanctions.

Obviously, some of these regimes will scramble in fear and issue platitudes about their opposition to terror, just as Arafat's Palestinian Authority, Iran, and Syria did, while they keep their terror apparatus intact. We should not be fooled. These regimes are already on the U.S. lists of states supporting terrorism—and if they are not, they should be.

The price of admission for any state into the coalition against terror first must be to dismantle completely the terrorist infrastructures within their realm. Iran will have to dismantle a worldwide network of terrorism and incitement based in Teheran. Syria will have to shut down Hizballah and the dozen terrorist organizations that operate freely in Damascus and in Lebanon. The Palestinians will have to crush Hamas and Islamic Jihad, close down their suicide factories and training grounds, break up the terrorist groups of Fatah and Tanzim, and cease the endless incitement to violence.

To win this war, we must fight on many fronts. The most obvious one is direct military action against the terrorists themselves. Israel's policy of preemptively striking at those who seek to murder its people is, I believe, better understood today and requires no further elaboration.

But there is no substitute for the key action that we must take: imposing the most punishing diplomatic, economic, and military sanctions on all terrorist states.

To this must be added these measures: Freeze financial assets in the West of terrorist regimes and organizations; revise legislation, subject to periodic renewal, to enable better surveillance against organizations inciting violence; keep convicted terrorists behind bars; refuse to negotiate with terrorists; train special forces to fight terror; and, not least important, impose sanctions on suppliers of nuclear technology to terrorist states.

I have had some experience in pursuing all these courses of action in Israel's battle against terrorism, including the sensitive matters surrounding intelligence.

But let me be clear: Victory over terrorism is not, at its most fundamental level, a matter of law enforcement or intelligence. However important these functions may be, they can only reduce the dangers, not eliminate them. The immediate objective is to end all state support for and complicity with terror. If vigorously and continuously challenged, most of these regimes can be deterred from sponsoring terrorism.

But there is a real possibility that some regimes will not be deterred—and those may be ones that possess weapons of mass destruction. Again, we cannot dismiss the possibility that a militant terrorist state will use its proxies to threaten or launch a nuclear attack with apparent impunity. Nor can we completely dismiss the possibility that a militant regime, like its terrorist proxies, will commit collective suicide for the sake of its fanatical ideology.

In this case, we might face not thousands of dead, but hundreds of thousands, and possibly millions. This is why the United States must do everything in its power to prevent regimes like Iran and Iraq from developing nuclear weapons, and to neutralize their use of other weapons of mass destruction.

This is the great mission that now stands before the free world. That mission must not be watered down to allow certain states to participate in the coalition that is now being organized. Rather, the coalition must be built around this mission.

It may be that some will shy away from adopting such

an uncompromising stance against terrorism. If some free states choose to remain on the sidelines, America must be prepared to march forward without them—for there is no substitute for moral and strategic clarity. I believe that if the United States stands on principle, all the democracies will eventually join the war on terrorism. The easy route may be tempting, but it will not win the day.

On September 11, I, like everyone else, was glued to a television set watching the savagery that struck America. Yet amid the smoking ruins of the Twin Towers one could make out the Statue of Liberty holding high the torch of freedom. It is freedom's flame that the terrorists sought to extinguish. But it is that same torch, so proudly held by the United States, that can lead the free world to crush the forces of terror and secure our tomorrow.

It is within our power. Let us now make sure that it is within our will.

FIGHTING TERRORISM

How Democracies Can Defeat
the International Terrorist Network

Preface

Terrorism is back—with a vengeance. After being subdued internationally and within most Western countries in the late 1980s, it has returned in ferocious and fearful new forms. In the United States, the bombings of the World Trade Center in Manhattan and the federal building in Oklahoma City demonstrated to Americans that terrorism could now strike on Main Street. Internationally, terrorist attacks from Beirut to Buenos Aires were recalling the familiar scenes of carnage from the 1980s on the television screens and front pages of the free world in the 1990s. In Paris, bombs exploded in a crowded subway after nearly a decade's respite from such outrages. And in Japan a horrifying new form of chemical terrorism struck fear in the hearts of millions of commuters in one of the world's most advanced societies.

Admittedly, the *modus operandi* of this new wave of terrorism is usually different from that of the earlier terrorism that afflicted the world for two decades beginning in the 1960s. The new terrorism boasts few, if any, hostage takings and practically no hijackings. It specializes in the bombing of its targets, and for good reason: The punishment meted out in the 1980s to hostage takers and airline hijackers, and to their sponsors, made the more overt kind of terrorism a costly affair. The new and not so new forces engaging in renewed terrorism seek to evade this punishment by hiding more deeply in the shadows than even their shadowy predecessors. Terrorism thrives in the dark and withers when stripped of its deniability. Yet it is a fact that today's domestic and international terrorists may be identified fairly easily, and it is therefore possible to deter and prevent them from pursuing the policies of terror.

I have been involved in the battle against terrorism for most of my adult life—first as a soldier in the special forces of the Israeli Army, then as one of the founders of an institute devoted to the study of terrorism, and later as a diplomat seeking to forge an alliance of the free nations in the active effort to defeat international terrorism. During the mid-1980s, I was part of a broad international effort to convince the citizens and leaders of the democratic nations that this terrorism could be stamped out. In 1986, I edited a book on anti-terror theory called *Terrorism: How the West Can Win*, which advanced an overall strategy for fighting the international terror which then raged around the globe. Within a short time, policymakers began recognizing that this terror could be defeated, and had to be forcefully confronted. Many of the principles in that book were adopted by the United

States, and after resolute action by the Reagan administration and other governments, international terrorism, thought invincible only a few years earlier, decidedly began to recede.

When I say that today's terrorism can be driven back as well, I do not mean to suggest that there are no hard decisions to be made along the way. Quite the contrary. The current breed of interlocking domestic and international terrorists is certainly not to be taken lightly. They know the West well and have developed strategies designed to take advantage of all its weaknesses. An effective battle against terrorism must of necessity require a shift in the domestic and international policies that enable terrorism to grow and the intensification of those efforts that can uproot it. Domestically in the United States, this requires a reassessment of the legal instruments necessary for combating homegrown terrorism, alongside the means to monitor added powers given to the government to pursue these ends. Internationally, this means identifying the great change that has taken place in the forces driving worldwide terrorism since the 1980s, and shaping a powerful international alliance against them.

Indeed, after an interlude of several years in which the vigil against terrorism was relaxed, new forces of domestic and international terror have emerged. Notable among the former are the runaway American militias of the "patriot movement," whose avowed goal is to prepare for a violent showdown with a "satanic" federal government; chief among the latter are the various strains of militant Islam, which likewise see their ultimate destiny as leading to a final confrontation with the Great Satan, the United States.

What this new terrorism portends for America and the world and what can be done about it has not yet been sufficiently understood. The growth of terrorism has been accompanied by a steady escalation in the means of violence, from small arms used to assassinate individuals, to automatic weapons used to mow down groups, to car bombs now capable of bringing down entire buildings, to lethal chemicals that (as in Japan) can threaten entire cities. The very real possibility that terrorist states and organizations may soon acquire horrific weapons of mass destruction and use them to escalate terrorism beyond our wildest nightmares has not been addressed properly by Western governments. It must be recognized that barring firm and resolute action by the United States and the West, terrorism in the 1990s will expand dramatically both domestically and internationally. Today's tragedies can either be the harbingers of much greater calamities yet to come or the turning point in which free societies once again mobilize their resources, their ingenuity, and their will to wipe out this evil from our midst Fighting terrorism is not a "policy option"; it is a neces sity for the survival of our democratic society and ou freedoms. Showing how this battle can be won is th purpose of this book.

I

The Plague of Domestic Terrorism

Organized crime has plagued all the democracies. It has attacked business establishments, assaulted judges, corrupted police officials. But the rise of terrorism in recent decades presents a new form of organized violence directed against democratic societies. Making their appearance in the late 1960s, terrorist attacks have afflicted virtually each of the Western countries in an unfailing sequence. The societies targeted have included Britain, Italy, France, Holland, Spain, Germany, Japan, Argentina, Israel, and most recently the United States itself. No country is immune, few are spared.

This new violence differs significantly from that of organized crime. While the violence of traditional organized crime is directed to achieving *financial* gains, terrorist violence, regardless of the specific identity and goals of its perpetrators, is always directed toward achieving *political* ends. Because of this distinction, the scope of the violence of organized crime is radically more limited. Gangsters kill only those they have to kill—usually other gangsters—in order to win or maintain control over specific areas of legal or illicit commerce. But terrorists are out to terrorize the public at large, with the intent of compelling some kind of change of policy, or else as retribution for the government's failure to follow the policies demanded by the terrorists.

This gets to the heart of what terrorism is, and how it differs from other kinds of violence. *Terrorism is the deliberate and systematic assault on civilians to inspire fear for political ends.* Though one may quibble with this definition, for example by broadening "political ends" to include ideological or religious motives, it nonetheless captures the essence of terrorism—the purposeful attack on the innocent, those who are *hors de combat,* outside the field of legitimate conflict. In fact, the more removed the target of the attack from any connection to the grievance enunciated by the terrorists, the greater the terror. What possible connection is there between the kindergarten children savaged in an office building in Oklahoma to the purported grievances of the Patriots of Arizona? What do the incidental shoppers bombed in the World Trade Center in Manhattan have to do with the Islamic *jihad*?

Yet for terrorism to have any impact, it is precisely the lack of connection, the lack of any possible involvement or "complicity" of the chosen victims in the cause the terrorists seek to attack, that produces the desired fear. For terrorism's underlying message is that every member of society is "guilty," that *anyone* can be a victim, and that therefore no one is safe.

Paradoxically, this all-encompassing characteristic of terrorist violence is also its undoing in democratic societies. The effect of fear is offset by an equal and often more powerful effect of revulsion and anger from the citizenry. By its very nature, the inhuman method chosen by the terrorists to achieve their aim disqualifies the aim from the start as one worthy of moral support. Though their professed purpose is invariably couched in the language of freedom and the battle for human rights, there is a built-in contradiction between such professed aims and the method chosen to implement them. In fact, the methods reveal the totalitarian strain that runs through all terrorist groups. Those who deliberately bomb babies are not interested in freedom, and those who trample on human rights are not interested in defending such rights. It is not only that the ends of the terrorists do not succeed in justifying the means they choose; their choice of means indicates what their true ends are. Far from being fighters for freedom, terrorists are the forerunners of tyranny. It is instructive to note, for example, that the French Resistance during World War II did not resort to the systematic killing of German women and children, although these were well within reach in occupied France. But in Cambodia, the Khmer Rouge showed no such restraint in their war against what they saw as the American-supported occupation. France, of course, is today a democracy; Cambodia is merely another one of the many despotisms where terrorists have come to power—and where they proceeded to carry out some of the most ghoulish crimes committed against humanity since World War II. Terrorists use the techniques of violent coercion in order to achieve a regime of violent coercion. They are undemocratic to the core, making use of the pluralism and freedom guaranteed by liberal societies in order to crush this very pluralism and freedom.

The citizens of free countries understand this instinctively. That is why the terrorists' message has limited sway in capturing a broad following from among the democratic citizenry of the society they attack. Thus the Baader-Meinhof faction seeking to build a new German society failed to win the hearts and minds of German youth; thus the Red Brigades failed to sway the masses in Italy; thus the Japanese Red Army remained an utterly marginal group. None of them ever gained the sympathy of the public at large, and remained restricted to a few hundred followers, sometimes a few dozen.

Compare this to the much more pervasive network of organized crime. Organized crime does not deal with the advancement of political ideas; it deals with the advancement of corruption, assisted by intimidation. It has many thousands of people on its payroll, and in some countries, most notably Italy, it penetrated all levels of society, up to members of the Cabinet. Graft requires no ideological persuasion. It speaks in the language of money, which is a universal tender, and therefore has wide appeal. This is why organized crime is so difficult to uproot, while most forms of terrorism in the democratic countries are relatively easy to stamp out.

This last statement needs to be examined, especially with regard to the United States. After all, America is the world's greatest democracy, and if terrorism cannot be successfully fought there, perhaps it is not a challenge as easily met as I have suggested. Indeed, in the rush of anxiety following the Oklahoma bombing, there was considerable concern in the United States that this bombing was a harbinger of a future wave of terrorist attacks against American society. It is true that the success of terrorism in one place often prompts imitation elsewhere, and in that regard it is not inconceivable that demented individuals and organizations will seek to replicate this tragedy. But I maintain that terrorism based exclusively in America is unsustainable and can be reduced to insignificance in short order—that over a few years at most, almost every one of these groups can be isolated, infiltrated, and disarmed.

The most important reason for this is the fact that the American public is by and large inoculated ideologically against the spread of the terrorist virus—that is, against the beliefs which motivate the terrorists. Such ideological inoculation can be seen in an example gleaned from a different field: Two former KGB agents said on the CBS program *60 Minutes*[1] that they worked for twenty years out of the Soviet embassy in Washington, yet failed to recruit even a single American citizen to spy against the United States. The only ones who did work for them were Americans who walked in unsolicited through the gates of the embassy, and their sole motivation was money. This reflects the basic patriotism of Americans and their widespread belief in the premises on which their society is built—unlike, say, many Soviet citizens who did not share such convictions about the Soviet Union during the years of the Cold War.

The belief in the peaceful resolution of disagreements, in the basic rights of other individuals, and in the law of the land—all these are the building blocks of a democratic education, indeed a democratic worldview, which forms an impenetrable wall in the mind of each citizen against participating in political violence. The possibility of persuading Americans that the indiscriminate bombing of other Americans is somehow going to be beneficial to the United States or the world is next to nil outside of the most lunatic fringe of society.

This fact flies directly in the face of one of the most infamous pieces of revolutionary wisdom ever uttered: Mao Ze-dong's theory that the irregular violence of his "people's army" could not be resisted because his men would simply disappear into the friendly and supportive populace, swimming among them "like the fish in the sea." This theory may have worked in China in 1949. Massacred, starved, impoverished, and oppressed, parts of the Chinese populace may very well have constituted such a sea that could provide the guerrillas with succor, cover, and moral support. Most proponents

12

of modern terrorism have liberally borrowed this theory, interchanging "terrorists" for "guerrillas," and suggesting that these, too, would be able to disappear into the friendly people's sea. But no such sea exists in the United States in 1995, nor in virtually any other democratic country today. The potential sympathizers willing to listen to the cynical theories of terrorist ideologists and collaborate with them in their grisly deeds do not constitute a "sea" but a collection of puddles at most.

The consequences of this reality for anti-terrorist law enforcement in a country like the United States are of the first order. For even in a nation as vast as America, the number of places in which any given terror initiative may be incubated or hatched is so small that it can usually be identifed with relative ease. Law enforcement officials know more or less whom to keep tabs on, and if they do not, the overwhelming majority of law-abiding citizens are willing and able to rapidly pool their knowledge and share it with the authorities. Thus within a day after the bombing in Oklahoma, federal investigators had literally *thousands* of leads offered them by ordinary citizens anxious to help. While the accused killer was apprehended by other means, the result of this public outpouring of support was that much of Timothy McVeigh's network of associates and potential supporters was laid bare to the scrutiny of both the police and the public within days.

While not every terrorist group can be located quite this quickly, it is nevertheless true that the Oklahoma

City bombers are not a needle in the haystack of American society; they are a needle in a bathtub, whose clear water ensures that their chances of hiding and getting away with their acts for very long is ordinarily exceedingly limited. One need only recall the short-lived exploits of the Symbionese Liberation Army (SLA), whose brief spate of murders and robberies received notoriety with the kidnapping of newspaper heiress Patty Hearst in 1974. The entire course of the SLA's violent history lasted just over a year. They were then forced into hiding and inactivity for several more months, until they were caught and wiped out by a Los Angeles Police Department SWAT team.

It can be argued, however, that the one-hundred-year history of the Ku Klux Klan refutes this proposition. The Ku Klux Klan, after all, engaged in violent attacks against black Americans and others. But the Klan was an outgrowth of the defeat of the Confederacy in the Civil War. It was formed in the late 1860s, in a society which was largely supportive of an often violent resistance against the liberalizing norms being imposed by the North. The Klan really was living in a sea of covert and overt sympathy, which sometimes reached as far as protection by local law enforcement officials—hence its longevity and its ability to muster not only terror but actual mass membership reaching millions at its height in the 1930s. But by the mid-1960s, the culture had changed in the new South, and the Klan's appeal dried out accordingly.

That is, until now. The investigation into the backgrounds of the suspects in the Oklahoma City bombing has led American law enforcement officials and journalists into a bewildering thicket of far-right, white supremacist and anti-federalist groups, often heavily armed, who in recent years have begun organizing themselves into local "militias"—in many cases actively planning to fight a civil war against the federal government. In this they vaguely echo the leftist anarchism of the minute Weathermen movement of the 1960s, but with a significant difference: Militia strength is now estimated to range from 10,000 to upward of 100,000, organized into a loose confederation with strongholds in thirty states, especially Montana, Idaho, Texas, Michigan, Indiana, and Florida. The fringes of the American right have always offered a certain support to anti-government groups such as the Ku Klux Klan, Posse Comitatus, and the Aryan Nations. In 1958, the John Birch Society was formed around the claims that the government was becoming dominated by Communist sympathizers, and arguing for limitations on the power of the federal government, the dismantling of the Federal Reserve System, and withdrawal from the United Nations. Periodically, radical splinters of this movement, from tax resisters to gun freaks, have had violent run-ins with federal agents. In 1983, for example, a member of the Posse Comitatus—a movement of agrarian tax resisters claiming the IRS was an arm of "Zionist international bankers"—wanted for the slaying of two U.S. marshals, was himself killed in a shoot-out with federal agents in Arkansas.

What makes this new "patriot movement" different is its ideological conviction that violent confrontation with what they view as a conspiratorial and authoritarian federal government has become inevitable—therefore making preparation for this conflict the duty of every true American patriot.

"Patriot" ideology appears to have taken a turn toward paranoia with President George Bush's 1990 announcement of his intention to forge a New World Order under the aegis of the United Nations (of which the Gulf War against Saddam Hussein was to be the first test). The idea that the United States would somehow be subordinated to the UN, an organization particularly hated and distrusted in "patriot" demonology, was enough to drive some in the fanatic fringe to distraction. Though Bush handily won the war against Iraq, this did not prevent the New World Order from promptly evaporating; international efforts led by the United States under the banner of the UN quickly fizzled out in Somalia and elsewhere. Yet the "patriots" remained convinced that America was in the throes of a great foreign conspiracy. A popular culture, in the form of apocalyptic anti-federal government novels such as William Pierce's *The Turner Diaries* and computerized bulletin boards on the Internet began spreading frantic warnings of the coming showdown with an American government controlled, variously, by one or more of the usual suspects: Russia, Zionism, and the United Nations—not to mention that perennial favor-

ite, the Trilateral Commission. What the entire genre
has in common is the belief in an imminent effort by
the federal government to seize private weapons, a belief which has reached fever pitch in the wake of two
events: the August 1992 Idaho shoot-out between re-
puted white separatist Randy Weaver and U.S. federal
agents, in which Weaver's wife and son lost their lives
along with a federal marshal, and the April 1993 attack
by the FBI on the Branch Davidian compound in
Waco, Texas, in which more than seventy cultists were
killed.

Following these actions, many of the militias concluded that civil war was coming, and began to say so.
Thus the Florida State Militia handbook warns: "We
have had enough . . . violence and bloodshed, enough
Waco . . . and government attacks on Christian Americans," and calls on its members to "buy ammo now.
You will not be able to get it later." Bo Gritz, who
founded an armed community in Idaho called Almost
Heaven, has called for the trial and execution of "the
traitors who ordered the assaults on the Weavers and
Waco." Samuel Sherwood of the United States Militia
Association in Idaho has preached that "civil war could
be coming, and with it the need to shoot Idaho legis-
lators." Norman Olson, leader of the Northern Michigan Regional Militia, understands "warfare, armed
rebellion" to be coming "unless the spirit of the country changes."[2] And it is these beliefs which have in the
last few years fueled an unprecedented explosion of

membership in these organizations, as thousands of sympathizers and fellow travelers have openly joined their ranks.

The language of militia and patriot ideology was exactly the kind of language used by Timothy McVeigh, the principal suspect in the Oklahoma City bombing, when he wrote in a letter in 1992 to the *Union Sun & Journal* of Lockport, New York, that the politicians had gone "out of control": "Do we have to shed blood to reform the current system? I hope it doesn't come to that. But it might."

None of the militias are willing to openly declare that the war with the United States has *already* started (much as Islamic radicals in the United States, whom I will discuss presently, are unwilling to state publicly that the *jihad* against the United States has already begun). None of them are willing to claim the Oklahoma City bombing as their own, although many profess to "understand the rage" which led to it. Many questions about the Oklahoma City bombing remain unanswered at the time of this writing, including who McVeigh's accomplices were and where he got the cash he used to plan his attack. What is clear is that in the heartland of America, the terrorist puddles are still puddles—but in the absence of forceful action by the government of the United States, there is the distinct danger that they will get larger and deeper.

Here one must be careful to maintain an important distinction between the xenophobia and bigotry of political extremism in the democracies, both on the left and on the right, and actual terrorism. Democracies always have their share of anti-immigrant or anti-establishment parties, as well as advocates of extreme nationalism or internationalism. Though such organizations—the French National Front is a good example—are unsavory in their views, they are often genuinely convinced participants in democracy, accepting its basic ground rules and defending its central tenets. These can and must be distinguished from the tiny splinters at the absolute fringes of democratic society, which may endorse many similar ideas but use them as a pretext to step outside the rubric of the democratic system to resort to violence and terror. The Ku Klux Klan, which is today attempting a political comeback in America, is forced to adopt softer tones in an attempt to squeeze in at the fringes of the legitimate spectrum. How far would the "new" Klan get if it turned out that it was still active in lynching innocent people in the night, or that it had taken up bombing buildings?

In short, American society at the close of the twentieth century still lacks a widespread and enduring social and cultural climate for the breeding of domestic terrorist organizations. It even lacks the pernicious chorus of intellectual rationalizers and legitimizers such as Jean-Paul Sartre and Frantz Fanon who gave European terrorism its short-lived flurry of faddish glamour when it first appeared. While there is a ready audience right now for instant experts expounding on the inevitable proliferation of domestic terrorism in America, the fact is that domestic terrorism has a bleak future in the United States, precisely because Americans—virtually *all* Americans—reject it out of hand.

Before I discuss the operational issues involved in defeating domestic terrorism, it is crucial to mention the battle of ideas which constitutes the first and most fundamental defense against terrorism. I have said that Americans, as profound believers in democracy and genuine lovers of their country, are for the most part inoculated against the ideas which are the wellspring of terrorism. But, as in the South of the Ku Klux Klan, it is clear that this was not always the case, and it would be foolish to think that the cultural resistance of Americans is necessarily permanent and undamageable. The intellectual bulwarks of a free society, like all aspects of freedom, have to be constantly nurtured and protected. In the case of the intellectual defense against the appeal of terrorism, the continual explication of democratic values is a fundamental requirement. That means first and foremost advancing the idea that the essence of democratic societies, and that which distinguishes them from dictatorships, is the commitment to resolve conflict in a nonviolent fashion by settling issues through argument and debate, and if the issue is important enough—through ballots rather than bullets.

As long as this ethos is widely maintained, democratic societies can cope with ethnic and social antagonisms, defusing their explosive potential and ultimately dissolving them. But when no such ethos is present, societies can descend into the most horrific bloodshed over almost any issue, as we have seen most recently in the monumental bloodlettings in Bosnia, Rwanda, Uganda, Somalia, and Algeria. While the Western democracies are thankfully nowhere near the condition of such countries, they, like all societies, have their frayed edges of unresolved grievances and violent alienation, which, if unattended, can serve as fertile soil for the growth of extremism and terrorism. The continual cultivation of democratic values throughout all levels of society is thus not a luxury or an abstract exercise but a crucial instrument for the survival and well-being of democratic countries.

The salient point that has to be underlined again and again is that *nothing* justifies terrorism, that it is evil *per se*—that the various real or imagined reasons proffered by the terrorists to justify their actions are meaningless. In its long and unfinished march from barbarism to civilization, humanity has tried to delineate limits to conflict. It has developed laws of war which proscribe, even in wartime, the initiation of deliberate attacks on defenseless civilians. Without this limitation there is no meaning to the term "war crimes." For if anything is allowable, then even the gassing of a million babies in Auschwitz and Dachau is also permissible. But by their uninhibited resort to violence and their repeated attacks on civilians, the terrorists brazenly cross the line between the permissible and the impermissible. By conditioning us to accept savage outrages as habitual or normal responses to undesired political circumstances, terrorism attacks the very foundations of civilization and threatens to erase it altogether by killing man's sense of sin, as Pope John Paul II put it. The unequivocal and unrelenting moral condemnation of terrorism must therefore constitute the first line of defense against its most insidious effect.

Yet it is precisely this defense that has been weakened by the rush to "explain" and "understand" the terrorists' motivations after the Oklahoma City bombing. A vast instant literature sprang forth seeking to explain the motivations and psychological makeup of America's newfound terrorists, just as a similar literature was produced at the height of European terrorism in the 1970s. A clinical understanding of terrorist psychology is of course important for fighting terrorism, but it must not spill over into the other connotation of understanding, that of acceptance. "Understanding" the personal hang-ups of Nazi leaders was perfectly justifiable as a means of advancing the total war against Nazism, but it never should have become an excuse to weaken the resolve for fighting Nazism as an absolute evil. The citizens of free societies must be told again and again that terrorists are savage beasts of prey, and should be treated as such. Terrorism should be given no intellectual quarter.

Like organized crime, the battle against terrorism should be waged relentlessly, resisting the attempt to glorify or mystify its perpetrators or their cause in any way. Indeed, the point of departure for the domestic battle against terrorism is to treat it as a *crime* and terrorists as *criminals*. To do otherwise is to elevate both to a higher status, thereby undermining the ability of governments to fight back. On the domestic level, the fact that terrorists are *politically* motivated criminals is irrelevant, except in providing clues for their apprehension.[3]

If the first obstacle to the spread of domestic terrorism in most democracies is in the realm of political culture, the second is in the realm of operations. The advanced democracies usually have at their disposal a vast array of surveillance and other intelligence-gathering capabilities that give them the ability to track down terrorists, put them on trial, and punish them. The United States is especially capable of monitoring the activities of terrorists. It has technical capabilities that exceed anything available to any other country, especially formidable eavesdropping and photographic capabilities. The movements and activities of potential terrorists can thus be observed, and they may be apprehended before they strike—at least when the law enforcement agencies are permitted to act.

A good example of just how powerful a national security agency can be in a democracy is provided by the case of the Federal Bureau of Investigation's crackdown which resulted in the elimination of the chief Puerto Rican terrorist group, the FALN. By 1982 the FALN had reached a peak of logistical capabilities, executing no fewer than twenty-five separate terrorist attacks including bombings of civilian targets and violent armed robberies. Additional and more ambitious attacks were in the works, including assaults on prisons in which

FALN members were being held. Yet eventually the FBI was able to catch up with the entire ring. It watched the movements of the group and literally listened in on its planning sessions for eighteen months. Finally, at the critical moment before a renewal of the terror spree, the FBI moved in and arrested four leaders of the group in the United States and tipped off the Mexican security services as to the location of a fifth. Without its head, the snake quickly expired, and by 1983 the FALN was unable to claim responsibility for a single terrorist act.

Evading the intelligence-gathering efforts of a democratic government is to a certain extent possible for a professionally organized terrorist organization. But the conditions for achieving this kind of capability are exacting. In order to maintain consistent, long-term terrorist activity in the face of massive counter-terrorist efforts that can be mounted by federal and local authorities, a terrorist group must have a number of assets at its disposal. First, its members must be exceptionally well trained in maintaining organizational secrecy and in the professional methods of covert operations and intelligence techniques. Second, it must be well funded and equipped, with the budgetary requirements of an effective terrorist organization rapidly running into the millions. And third, it must have a safe haven in and out of which its operatives can maneuver in their efforts to dodge the government's security services.

In the advanced democracies, none of these requirements is easy to meet, and for the same reasons that recruitment of terrorists is so difficult. Unwanted by the American public, the terrorists have neither the support of government officials who, in a non-democratic society, might share intelligence information with them or fail to take the necessary actions against them—they generally do not have a significant enough backing among citizens who are sympathetic and willing to help fund their activities—nor any piece of territory that has any kind of depth as a home base. In a modern democracy, the terrorist is most often alone, hunted, despised, and without means. Thus, the situation could in principle be created in which the terrorist would sooner or later succumb to the sophistication and sheer volume of activities against him.

II

The Question of Civil Liberties

If the chances of waging a campaign of domestic terrorism against a modern democracy are in theory marginal, there is a catch: The major democracies, although eminently capable of fighting terror effectively, are often hesistant to do so. To understand why, it is important to recognize that there are two kinds of strategies for fighting domestic terror. The first is a system of *passive* security, in which many of the potential targets of terrorists are "hardened" against a potential attack, both for deterrence and to actually blunt the effects of a possible assault. This involves the extensive use of watchmen and undercover security personnel, careful scrutiny of all individuals approaching likely targets such as government facilities and the public transportation system, on-site security systems, and heightened alertness of the civilian population. In Israel, much of the adult population are army reservists in combat units, and many of them also carry small arms, further increasing the difficulty of ex-

ecuting a successful terror attack. Such measures have the
advantage that they are relatively unobtrusive, having
next to no consequences for the civil liberties of the citizens, who are merely better prepared for an attack that
may come.

But while passive measures against terror may be par-
tially effective in a small country such as Israel, they are
of only limited use in a vast nation like the United States,
which has thousands of airports and tens of thousands of
federal buildings strewn throughout the fifty states. The
symbols of national authority are accordingly more dif-
fuse by order of magnitude, and the potential sites where
spectacular damage can be done are nearly infinite. Con-
versely, the security services, unlike those of the authoritarian regimes, are extremely limited in number, the FBI
commanding no more than 11,000 men. As was demonstrated by the bombing of the federal building in
Oklahoma City, the terrorists can strike at any one of an
unlimited number of possible targets, and the government has no hope of adequately protecting them all. In
order to defend such an immense and complex society
against terrorism—and the same must be said of other
major democracies, such as Britain, France, and Germany—there is little choice but to adopt an *active* posture
against terror, taking the initiative to put into use the
overwhelming technological and logistical advantages in
the hands of law enforcement agencies. This means actively identifying the "puddles" from which terrorist activity is likely to emerge, monitoring the activities of

groups and individuals which advocate violence, analyzing and pooling intelligence on their nature, goals, and technical capacity for violence, and employing preemptive surveillance, search and seizure, interrogations, detentions, and prosecutions when it becomes apparent that planning for terrorist violence is taking place.

Against such active anti-terror activities, the amateur practitioners of domestic terrorism, unschooled in the arts of covert action, do not stand a chance. But the trouble with such active anti-terror activities is that, unlike passive measures, they *do* constitute a substantial intrusion on the lives of those who are being monitored. Steeped as they are in moral and legal respect for the privacy of the individual, Western democracies have been hesitant—and justifiably so—to embark on activities which remind them too much of the doings of the authoritarian states they so abhor. Indeed, every one of the active steps that a democratic state can take against domestic terrorists constitutes a certain curtailment of *someone's* freedom to speak, assemble, or practice his religion without interference. One need only consider the activities involved in building a domestic terrorist organization to recognize that these groups invariably engage in incitement, pamphleteering, and indoctrination toward their purposes, and gather to lay plans and prepare for their execution. In some cases, the incitement is also of a religious or quasi-religious nature—as in the cases of abortion-clinic bombers and Islamic advocates of *jihad,* Islamic holy war. And it is just these kinds of speech, assembly, and religious expression which, if properly monitored, give law enforcement agencies the warning they need in order to head off calamity.

The governments of free societies charged with fighting a rising tide of terrorism are thus faced with a democratic dilemma: If they do not fight terrorism with the means available to them, they endanger their citizenry; if they do, they appear to endanger the very freedoms which they are charged to protect.

In the United States, such freedoms are more scrupulously protected than in any other country in the world, and there are even some who claim that free speech and religious freedom should be considered "absolute" rights. While even the most passionate advocates of civil liberties concede, along with Supreme Court Justice Oliver Wendell Holmes, that freedom of expression must stop at "shouting 'fire' in a crowded theater," American law has thus far been rigidly resistant to limiting the scope of such exceptions. Just how far the concern with free speech has gone was driven home to me in a recent conversation with a security expert who explained the constraints imposed on the FBI by the Attorney General's guidelines which govern monitoring activities: They prohibit law enforcement officials from using government funds to so much as buy a newsletter by a militant group in order to examine it for threats of terrorist activity—and if an official were to pay for the newsletter out of his own pocket, he would be prohibited from storing the clippings in a government office, because such rudimentary intelligence gathering is considered an "infringement" on the liberties of the groups involved.

The guidelines, instituted as a reaction to federal activities in the Vietnam War era, permit the FBI to engage in "investigations" of crimes committed in the past or crimes presently being planned. But in the long run, each criminal investigation produces only a tiny part of the picture of extremist organization and political violence in the United States; the total is no more than a collection of fragments. At present, the FBI is not allowed to perform the most basic intelligence activities required for piecing together the puzzle of political ideology, incitement, infrastructure, and paramilitary organization which, once assembled, could lead to an understanding of where the most deadly terrorism is *likely* to come from. Such monitoring could possibly have led to an early identification of the Patriots of Arizona as a probable trouble spot, and might even have prevented the tragedy in Oklahoma City; without it, the FBI is a blinded Samson, fit to fight but incapable of seeing its enemies.

An example of how domestic intelligence work such as that forbidden to the FBI has made all the difference in the European counter-terror effort was provided by Christian Lochte, former head of the Office for the Protection of the Constitution, the branch of the German security services responsible for anti-terror activities. In December 1982, a neo-Nazi terrorist group embarked on a campaign of bombings against the cars of American GIs, eventually turning on Israeli targets in Vienna, Am-

sterdam, and Geneva. Lochte reports that at first the security services were baffled by the attacks, since they
seemed to be part of the neo-Nazi terrorism which had
spawned attacks like the 1980 bombing of the Munich
Oktoberfest, which had claimed thirteen lives. But while
some of the existing neo-Nazi groups had clearly begun
to practice terror against German targets, their association with attacks against American servicemen could not
be explained by any of the information available from
previous crimes. The key to the mystery was found in
an ideological tract published in 1982 by two West
German radicals, Walter Hexel and Odfried Hepp, entitled *Farewell to Hitlerism*. In it, Hexel and Hepp re-
nounced the traditional Nazi hostility toward Soviet
Communism, identifying American imperialism as a hostile occupying force from which West Germany had to
be freed through a "liberation struggle" by a renewed
Nazism. The idea of an anti-Western Nazism sympathetic to the Soviet Union eventually led to the identification of Hexel and Hepp as the leaders of a new
terrorist group, which was eventually found to have been
trained in Lebanon by the Soviet-sponsored PLO and to
have mounted the attacks in collusion with Abul Abbas's
Palestine Liberation Front faction.[1]

Of course, there is something laudable in the efforts
of Western democracies to hold their governments to
the highest possible standards when it comes to respect-
ing the rights of their citizens—including not having
intelligence gathered about them. From the days of
Robespierre's infamous Committee for Public Safety,

democracies have had to guard against this danger, couched in terms of national security, which unduly invades the privacy of each citizen in the name of national security. Yet the threat to the basic civic rights of *not* fighting terrorism are even more debilitating to a free society. We often forget the monstrous violation of personal rights which is the lot of the *victims* of terror and their families, or the wholesale violation of the rights of entire citizenries when they are forced to expend time and resources to protect themselves against potential terrorist attacks—not to mention the more subtle violation of basic human rights involved when a person, or an entire people, must learn to live in fear.

The belief that freedom of speech and religion are absolutes that cannot be compromised even in the slightest way out of very real security concerns is merely tantamount to replacing one kind of violation of rights with another, even worse violation of those same rights. It is evident that such terror-inflicted violations of the civil rights of a people may, if attacks are an extraordinary rarity, be insufficient to justify taking any kind of serious action; but it is equally evident that there is some point at which terror becomes by far the bigger threat to citizens' rights and the time comes to take unflinching action. In this regard, there is apparently a moment of truth in the life of many modern democracies when it is clear that the unlimited defense of civil liberties has gone too far and impedes the protection of life and liberty, and governments decide to adopt active measures against the forces that menace their societies. In Britain, that moment came in 1973, after IRA violence had reached unprecedented heights. That year the British Parliament passed an Emergency Provisions Act, providing for arrest, search and seizure without a warrant, relaxed rules of evidence, trials conducted by lone judges (to avoid intimidated juries), and outlawing membership in a terrorist organization. For Germany, the moment of truth came in 1976, with the kidnapping and murder of the industrialist Hans Martin Schleyer by the Baader-Meinhof group. The result was a revolution in German criminal law giving the security services an extended right of detention without warrant, as well as a substantial removal of constraints on search and seizure. For Italy, the moment came in 1978, with the abduction and murder of former Prime Minister Aldo Moro, which led the Italians to give their security services powers similar to those adopted in Germany, plus a special amnesty law allowing terrorists to turn themselves in and become state's witnesses. In France, a spree of bombings by Hizballah in the mid-1980s at the Galeries Lafayette, the Place de l'Opéra, the Champs-Elysées and other centers of cultural life led to a build-up of passive defenses so thick that parts of Paris had at times begun to look like an army encampment. Finally, in 1986, the French reached their moment of truth and moved to an active anti-terror policy that led to the elimination of that terrorist threat on French soil.

In fact, the record of active anti-terror techniques, once adopted, has been excellent. In the wake of active anti-terror action by democratic governments in the 1970s and

1980s, the most notorious of European domestic terrorist groups were eliminated one by one, including the Baader-Meinhof, the German Red Army Faction, the Italian Red Brigades, Action Directe in France, and Germany's bizarre anti-Western neo-Nazi terrorist cells. Thus Europe was for the most part freed of the plague of domestically grown terrorism. Lethal IRA terrorism, while not eliminated, was reduced by more than 80 percent.[2]

Most recently, it was Japan that faced a potentially disastrous domestic terrorist threat and moved swiftly to overcome it. The attempt by an obscure cultist group Aum Shinrikyo to poison Tokyo's congested subways with sarin—one of the most toxic chemicals ever developed—was not the first time Japan had to deal with Japanese-bred terrorists. The Japanese Red Army, whose heyday was in the 1970s, had been a terrorist group directed primarily *outward*. Cooperating openly with the PLO, and less openly as well with European terrorist factions, most of its attacks were carried out beyond Japan's borders. The Japanese powers therefore did not apply their full weight against the group, and did not in any way test the limits of Japan's democratic institutions in fighting it. Japan's Red Army withered as the pro-Soviet terror axis of which it was a part disintegrated, eventually all but disappearing under less than overwhelming pressure from the Japanese government.

Yet in 1995 Japan found itself facing a much more immediate terrorist threat. As in any other land, Japanese culture occasionally breeds wild offshoots of what could be called Japanese fundamentalists—private militias centered around charismatic leaders who use terrorism and violence to bring a straying Japan back to the "pure" ways of an older order. Well remembered is the warrior group of the celebrated ultra-nationalist novelist Yukio Mishima, who in 1970 attempted a takeover of the government as unfeasible as it was public, only to commit suicide before the watching eyes of his nation. The sarin attack was of course a far more serious event, drawing the attention of the world because of the extraordinary deadliness of the menace. Although it failed to produce the mass catastrophe that had been planned, it became immediately clear that without the most determined action, the next attack could indeed succeed in bringing about the deaths of thousands. Faced with this contingency, the Japanese government did what it had failed to do in the past. It used every power available to it, including unlimited surveillance and an aggressive sweep of searches and seizures. Results quickly followed: The group's leader was located and placed under arrest, the group's weapons' caches and poison factories uncovered—along with two tons of chemicals and over $7 million in cash—and its thousands of members all but neutralized as a challenge to Japanese society. Japan, like many democracies before it, had reached its moment of truth—and acted.

While the United States and Canada have been hesitant to follow the lead of the European states and Japan in moving against their terrorist enemies at home, this is not to say the great democracies on the western side of the Atlantic have had no experience with a more aggressive anti-terror policy. In 1970 Canada was faced with a spate of domestic terror at the hands of the Quebecois Liberation Front (FLQ), a tiny separatist group which got as far as blowing up a plane. The Canadians responded by invoking the War Measures Act of 1942, granting extensive emergency powers to the security services, which in short order reduced the FLQ to a memory. Looking back, we can see that it was this quick and draconian action which stamped out domestic terrorism in Canada for decades to come.

Perhaps the most striking example in which the United States was forced to momentarily curtail civil liberties in the face of potential terrorist activity occurred during the Gulf War. When Saddam Hussein invaded Kuwait in the summer of 1990, Iraq was by no means a world military power, and Saddam's chances of winning a conventional war were slim. But Saddam had several cards up his sleeve that he believed might be able to make the Americans think twice. One was his arsenal of Scud missiles and chemical-weapons stockpiles, which he claimed to be willing to use to "incinerate half of Israel," thereby hoping to shift the focus of the war to an Arab–Israeli confrontation and splitting the Arab partners in the international coalition arrayed against him; the other was terror, which he threatened to loose against the United States and its allies in the event of a counteroffensive in Kuwait. Indeed, there was every reason to think that Saddam would be able to make good on his threats. Iraq had long been one of the foremost sponsors of international terrorism, hosting in Baghdad such terrorist groups as the Abu Nidal organization, Abul Abbas's Palestine Liberation Front (PLF), and the organization of the notorious bomb maker Abu Ibrahim. Yasir Arafat's PLO, which had an extensive network of operatives among Palestinian Arabs residing in Kuwait, provided Saddam with valuable intelligence which he used in planning the invasion, and there was a danger that the PLO would join in conjuring up an unprecedented wave of anti-Western mayhem at Saddam's behest. Other pro-terror states, such as Sudan and Yemen, supported Saddam as well. Indeed, of all the central sponsors of international terrorism then active, only Syria refrained from supporting Iraq's promised "mother of all wars"—out of a neighborly interest in seeing Saddam toppled, and in exchange for billions of dollars in Saudi money brokered by the American government.

While most people are aware of the results of Saddam's missile attacks against Israel—thirty-nine barrages against Tel Aviv and other Israeli cities resulted in only a single death from the actual bombardment—less is remembered about the terrorist front of the war against Saddam. Even before the war, the American intelligence community recognized that with the majority of the world's terrorist networks poised to assault Western targets, the Allied invasion of Kuwait could easily end up being a costly affair even if the Allied troops won the land and air battles handily. There was no viable option of passive defense against the terrorists, and the Bush administration concluded that there was no choice but to follow the Europeans' lead and adopt a more activist policy. It ordered "a crackdown on all potential sources of threat," which included surveillance, searches, interrogations, and expulsions en masse of Iraqi diplomats, PLO operatives, and other potential agents of Iraqi terror. For possibly the first time in decades, a concerted anti-terror effort was conducted simultaneously by the governments of virtually every democratic nation. And the result was an unambiguous victory for the Western security services. Of 173 terrorist attacks during the weeks of the Gulf War, 143 took place in Third World and Arab countries; the terrorists were able to pull off a total of only thirty attacks against the principal enemy, the Western countries, and these were for the most part unsuccessful, inflicting no more than ten deaths among them. In this way, the promised threat of fearful terror directed against the United States and its allies was quietly reduced to irrelevance.[3]

A grisly postscript to this story took place in Greece, where students expelled from the country on suspicion of being a security threat were allowed to return the month after the end of the war—only to blow themselves up in a post office in the college town of Patras, while trying to mail a package bomb to the British legation. Seven people were killed in the blast. The "students" were members of the Islamic Jihad Brigades, one of the six known factions of the Islamic Jihad; this one an organ of the "Western Sector" terror apparatus in Yasir Arafat's Fatah.

What these examples show is that domestic terrorism—and, as we have just seen, under certain conditions international terrorism as well—can be controlled, reversed, or defeated outright by the democratic nations. There is no question that the United States has the political culture and operational capacity to eviscerate domestic terror. The question is whether it has yet reached that same moment of truth which brought the major Western European countries to allow their security services to take the vigorous action needed to uproot the terror in the midst of their societies.

The basic barrier to such action in the United States is essentially one of political philosophy and jurisprudence. Some Americans fear that an active anti-terror strategy would compromise the free, democratic nature of American society. Yet in none of the democracies has the adoption of firm anti-terror measures led to a significant or lasting curtailment of individual freedoms. It did require, however, the explicit revision of the widespread conviction that a democratic society can guarantee the freedoms of speech, assembly, religion, the bearing of arms, diplomatic immunity, and political asylum—as if they were practically absolutes. They are not and cannot be absolutes, as the record of terrorist abuse of these democratic freedoms demonstrates again and again. The fact is that both the primary co-conspirators in the World Trade Center bombing entered the United States as political refugees—one from Iraq and the other claiming he had been oppressed in Israel (both would have most likely received political asylum had they not spoiled their chances by blowing up a building). More bizarre is the fact that a *fatwah* (Islamic legal ruling) ordering the death of Salman Rushdie for having written *The Satanic Verses* is—incredibly—being preached in the United States as "protected" speech, shielded by an absurdly generous interpretation of "freedom of speech and religion." Still more disturbing is the utterly excessive American generosity in interpreting the "right" to bear arms as including freedom from practically any kind of licensing and government supervision, a freedom well abused by David Koresh's militaristic messianic Branch Davidian cult in its incendiary confrontation with federal agents in Waco, Texas, in 1993, leaving scores dead. In the absence of countervailing legislation, other ultra-nationalist "militia" and neo-Nazis continue to conduct battalion-level exercises in barely veiled preparation for coming military action against the American government, of the sort which produced the Oklahoma City bombing, and yet their activities, too, are considered constitutionally "protected."

A good example of the absurdity of shielding terrorist incitement is provided by the case of Sheikh Omar Abdel Rahman, the blind Egyptian cleric whose Gamaa Islamiya terror network has been charged with the World Trade Center bombing and with planning attacks on targets such as the Lincoln Tunnel. Rahman was allowed into the United States in 1990 from Sudan, after a history of perfidy in his native land, which included serving time for recruiting members for the Islamic terrorist faction that had assassinated President Anwar Sadat. His *fatwahs* in Egypt and the United States are among the bloodiest ever issued, calling for the death of Sadat's successor, Hosni Mubarak, and the overthrow of the Egyptian regime, and ruling in favor of the murder of foreign tourists traveling in Egypt. Yet none of this was sufficient to justify the scrutiny of the American authorities, because Rahman's freedom of action in the United States was protected by the right to immigrate into the country and, once there, the right to practice his brand of freedom of speech and religion, which called for outright murder. It was only *after* Rahman's minions had already killed five and had injured hundreds in the Twin Towers in Manhattan that some of those rights were curbed. It is clear that a fresh look is needed at the way the United States presently chooses which liberties are worthy of protection.

The ideal of an absolute civil liberty—whether a "leftist" liberty such as absolute free speech or a "rightist" liberty such as the absolute right to bear arms—should be tempered by political realities, and the attempt to apply it in its pristine form has grave consequences. When a society tries to grant such pockets of unlimited freedom, it provides the proverbial 99 percent of normal citizens with supposed "rights" that they neither want nor need—the "right" to call for the murder of what they deem an obnoxious author, or the "right" to own a grenade launcher. But there are always those in the other 1 percent who, if granted such freedoms, *are* capable of coming up with ways to abuse them. In fact, it is just such supposed rights that are needed to transform a handful of odious but essentially impotent lunatics at the edges of society into a seething menace capable of turning that society into a shambles. Advocates of absolute civil liberties forget that legally protected freedoms are not *ends* in and of themselves; they are *means* to ensuring the health and well-being of the citizens. The United States Constitution, said Justice Robert Jackson, is not a suicide pact. And when a protected "right" in practice results in the encouragement and breeding of terrorist monstrosities ready to devour other members of society, then it is clear that such a right has ceased to serve its true end and must be either revised or reduced.

At the Jonathan Institute's 1979 conference, Professor Joseph W. Bishop of Yale University inquired into the question of whether the United States Constitution could be made to square with firm anti-terror measures such as had been adopted in Britain, Germany, and other European democracies. After all, the Fifth Amendment of the U.S. Constitution appears to prohibit convictions on the basis of self-incriminating testimony—which is just the kind that security services are practiced in obtaining in interrogation; it similarly prohibits depriving a citizen of his liberties without "due process of law"—which is exactly what an arrest without a warrant is; the Sixth Amendment guarantees the right to a trial by jury—and yet the British found trials by a lone judge to be a crucial step in obtaining convictions, because the Ulster citizenry had become so intimidated by terrorists.

Yet Bishop's conclusion was that even under the rigid civil liberties orientation of the American Bill of Rights, the courts had consistently upheld the authority of the executive branch to curtail civil freedoms where there was compelling evidence of a threat to the security of the United States if these unlimited liberties remained in force. Thus Bishop notes that the Supreme Court, which is responsible for ensuring that the government of the United States conforms to the standards set out in the Constitution, stood aloof as Abraham Lincoln dramatically curtailed civil liberties during the Civil War. Lincoln suspended the writ of *habeas corpus*, had civilians in the South tried by military tribunals without the use of either a jury or the normal rules of evidence, and made use of wholesale internment of individuals suspected of supporting the Confederacy—and yet the Supreme Court was silent. The Court also refrained from commenting on the so-called Ku Klux Klan Act of 1871, which gave the President virtually unlimited power to suppress the activities of the Klan "by using the militia or the armed forces, or both, *or by any other means*, to take such measures as he considers necessary to suppress ... any insurrection, domestic violence ... or conspiracy" which—like terrorism—prevents citizens from enjoying their legal rights. During World War II, the Supreme Court upheld the military trial of American civilians suspected of engaging in activities on behalf of the Nazis and even the dreadful mass internment of Japanese-Americans for the duration of the war.[4]

As these examples strongly suggest, the American judicial system is ready and able to distinguish normal, peaceful circumstances from those in which the security of American citizens is being threatened by organized violence from without or within. This willingness to take responsibility and make hard decisions in the service of democracy is the hallmark of a mature political culture, such as the American Founding Fathers hoped would evolve in the United States. As James Madison wrote to Thomas Jefferson with regard to the balance between the powers of the state and the rights of the citizen: "It is a melancholy reflection that liberty should be equally exposed to danger whether the government have too much or too little power."[5] However, when it came to matters that endangered the security of the nation, Madison and Alexander Hamilton were unequivocal that the authority of the executive to ensure the security of the nation must take precedence over *all* other concerns. As they wrote in *The Federalist*:

[The powers to ensure security] ought to exist without limitation, because it is impossible to foresee or to define the extent and variety of national exigencies, and the correspondent extent and variety of the means which may be necessary to satisty them. The circumstances that endanger the safety of nations are infinite, and for this reason no constitutional shackles can be wisely imposed on the power to which the care of it is committed.

... As I know nothing to exempt this portion of the globe from the common calamities that have befallen other parts of it, *I acknowledge my aversion to every project that is calculated to disarm the government of a single weapon, which in any possible con-*

tingency might be usefully employed for the general defense and security [emphasis mine].

As the constitutional scholar Walter Berns pointed out at the Jonathan Institute's 1984 conference, even a great defender of democracy like Abraham Lincoln was forced to assume extraordinary powers when the security of the American nation was in jeopardy. Among his other encroachments on civil liberties which he deemed to be endangering the United States, he authorized the execution by firing squad of those who used their freedom of speech to demoralize the Union armies and incite criminal defections. His justification was that in impinging on the rights of the agitator, he protected the rights of the rest of society: "Must I shoot a simple-minded soldier boy who deserts, while I must not touch a hair of a wily agitator who induces him to desert? . . . I think that, in such a case, to silence the agitator and save the boy is not only constitutional, but a great mercy." What distinguishes Lincoln's case from our case today, in which the idea of curtailing freedom of speech in order to protect the United States is so difficult for many to accept? According to Berns, the answer is that Lincoln truly believed that the survival of the society he deeply cherished was in jeopardy. Lincoln called America "the last best hope of earth"—and meant it. And valuing the unique society that had been built there, he could not find the rationale to grant those who did not value it the freedoms that would enable them to destroy it.[6]

The terrorism of today has obviously in no way

reached the dimensions of the Civil War in jeopardizing the United States. Nor can we disregard the natural development of the concept of civil liberties over the intervening century. But the unchecked growth of terrorism is a grave danger in and of itself. Rampant terrorism is a mortal threat to any society. Of course, the need to cut back on the absolute freedom of the terrorist, a freedom which ultimately undermines democracy, does not by any means mean that law enforcement agencies should be granted absolute freedom either. As always in forging a legal system, the key is in striking a judicious compromise.

In the European democracies, two methods have been developed for ensuring that the executive branch's efforts against terrorism remain within the bounds of the legitimate effort to save lives. The British model, which dates back to 1973 and the beginning of intensified terrorism by the new Irish Republican Army (IRA), controls the activities of the security services by requiring that they annually receive a new legislative mandate from Parliament. Thus, the burden of proof lies with law enforcement officials to demonstrate that their special powers are justified and under control; failure to do so means the automatic expiration of their license to act. On the Continent, on the other hand, the responsibility for keeping an eye on the activities of the security services is usually concentrated in the hands of the judicial system, which reviews anti-terror actions to make sure that they can be justified out of legitimate concerns for public safety, generally within a specified number of days. Requiring periodic renewal of a legislative mandate and judicial review within a prescribed period permits the public, through its elected representatives and judges, to monitor the activities of its monitors.

But perhaps the most important factor in regulating the conduct of counter-terrorism by democratic governments is the independent investigative powers of the free press—and the right of the citizens to turn their government out of power if they feel it has gone too far. Presumably a public recognizing that the govenment had begun to slide down the road to oppression through reckless violations of civil rights would in short order find somebody more respectful of its interests. Yet the history of European counter-terrorism reveals no such public reaction, and for good reason. In Britain, Germany, Italy, and France, such active measures have had next to no adverse effects on the civil liberties of the overwhelming majority of citizens, a fact which is emphasized by the lack of any democratic backlash worth mentioning. These countries remain perfectly and fully democratic in every way—but their citizens feel more secure as a result of responsible government efforts to ensure that those inciting and preparing for political violence are kept at bay.

Both experience and common sense suggest, then, that the fascist and Marxist theory that democracies are weak and incapable of defending themselves against the superior ideological motivation of their terrorist opponents is groundless. Indeed, the exact reverse is true: The Western democracies are inherently very strong, precisely due to the nearly universal ideological ties which, beneath the cacophony of democratic politics, quietly unite their peoples. It is the terrorists who are in fact weak, resorting to bombs only because they can get no one to listen to them in any other fashion. It only remains to a democratic society to *decide* that it is willing to use the tools at its disposal to eliminate the scourge of domestic terror, and this end can be achieved with astonishing speed.

It is natural that a society of free citizens should shrink before a path which inevitably involves limiting the very liberties which the society is committed to protect. For granting extensive security powers to law enforcement officials in a vast nation is impossible without encountering a certain number of abuses as well. And while such abuses may be relatively unimportant during wartime or when the terror threat appears to be entirely out of control, it is also natural that when the authorities get the upper hand and the threat recedes somewhat, the relative importance of every abuse will grow again, raising the demand for more careful oversight of the security services. Thus it seems that the democracies are destined to wander to and fro between the poles of too much liberty and too extensive a security effort, walking the fine line between security and freedom. But so long as the tension between these two poles is maintained, without one extreme becoming the permanent fixation of the society and its ruin, the democracies can hope to have the best of both, remaining at once free and secure.

The prospect of constantly being jostled by the swings of this pendulum is not all that pleasant, but it is not that bad either. And as America stands before the crucial decision to embark on a path that many other mature democracies have had to take, it must bear in mind Spinoza's great injunction. No thinker was more important in laying the philosophical foundations of the modern democratic state, yet in his *Theological-Political Treatise,* Spinoza was careful to define clear limits to personal freedoms, including the pivotal one of freedom of speech, without which the meaning of democracy is vitiated. "We cannot deny that [the] authority [of the state] may be as much injured by words as by actions; hence . . . [the] unlimited concession [of free speech] would be most baneful . . ." Those kinds of speech which should not be permitted are "those which by their very nature nullify the [social] compact . . ."[7]

We need not adopt Spinoza's particular prescription regarding which kinds of speech are to be regulated in order to preserve democracy. But we should recognize the larger principle that he is articulating: that civil liberties should sometimes be limited not only at the point when physical violence is actually being perpetrated against others but also when such action is being incited, planned, and organized. That is, democracies have a right and a duty to protect themselves in advance against those who would set out to destroy their societies and extinguish their freedoms.

III

The 1980s: Successes Against International Terrorism

The Western democracies are capable of eliminating the domestic terror in their midst only if they decide to make use of the operational tools presently at their disposal. But such optimism would be misplaced with regard to international terrorism, a much hardier and more implacable nemesis. What road should the United States and other democracies pursue if they are to overcome not only the domestic terror of Oklahoma City but the potentially much more insidious international terror which produced the World Trade Center bombing, and which may very well produce other such tragedies before it has been defeated? To answer this question, we must first understand the nature and genesis of international terrorism and the process by which it has assumed its present form.

International terrorism is the use of terrorist violence against a given nation *by another state*, which uses the terrorists to fight a proxy war as an alternative to conventional war. Sometimes the terror is imported at the initiative of a foreign movement which nevertheless enjoys the support of a sovereign state, at the very least in the form of a benign passivity which encourages the growth of such groups on its own soil. The reason that international terrorism is so persistent and so difficult to uproot is that the support of a modern state can provide the international terrorist with everything that the domestic terrorist usually lacks in the way of cultural and logistical assistance. An alien, non-democratic society may be able to provide the depth of support for terrorist ideas to spawn a genuine terrorist army; it can offer professional training and equipment for covert operations, as well as diplomatic cover and other crucial logistical aid; it can make available virtually unlimited funds; and most important of all, it can ensure a safe haven to which the terrorists may escape and from which they can then emerge anew. Thus, with the support of a terrorist state, the terrorist is no longer a lonely and hunted fugitive from society. He becomes part of a different social milieu, which encourages him, nurtures him, protects him, and sees to it that he succeeds. The absurdly lopsided contest between the Western security services and the terrorist is under these circumstances no longer lopsided. It now pits the formidable resources of the West against the nearly comparable resources of a foreign state or network of states—and in this contest it is by no means immediately clear who will emerge the victor.

As late as 1979, when my colleagues and I had organized one of the first conferences on international terrorism, there were still many who did not recognize that there was such a thing as *international* terror. The wild growth of terrorism against the United States and virtually every one of its allies over the preceding two decades was often understood to be the result of a proliferation of technology, which had suddenly permitted "frustrated" individuals to become much more effective in expressing domestic social outrage that had always been there. At the time, many of the journalists attending the conference, and even some of the participants, believed that the support of states for terrorism was an incidental phenomenon, and that its essence lay in the domestic causes that "spontaneously" generated the violence.

But it was nothing of the sort. As has by now been revealed in the wake of the collapse of Soviet Communism in 1989, most of the international terror that plagued the world from the late 1960s through the mid-1980s was the product of an *ad hoc* alliance between the Soviet bloc and dictatorial Arab regimes. Together, these two groups of states sponsored or supported most of the international terrorist activities that took place during this period.

The proclivity toward terror on the Soviet side had clearly defined origins. The philosophical roots of European and Soviet terrorism may be traced to an anti-czarist group called Narodnaya Volya, or The People's Will, which in 1879 began a campaign which eventually succeeded in killing Czar Alexander II as a representative of the autocratic, capitalist, Russian Orthodox social system which was to be destroyed in its entirety. The success of subsequent domestic terrorists, such as the Social Revolutionaries (SR), in breaking down the prestige of the czarist government and preparing the way for the revolution taught the Bolshevik leadership the utility and importance of the terrorist method in destabilizing and eventually destroying regimes.[1] When Soviet Communism finally emerged as an international power in 1945, after the defeat of Germany, it was these indelible memories which became one of the underlying motifs of Soviet foreign policy. In the 1940s and 1950s, the Soviet Union and its satellite regimes trained insurgents and assassins from Italy, Greece, French Indochina, and Portuguese Africa in terrorist methods.

Italy provides a telling example of how the Soviet terrorist network operated. Marxist assassins in Italy were already receiving training in the Soviet satellite states of Czechoslovakia and the former Yugoslavia in the period immediately following World War II. By the close of the 1940s, a terrorist group called Volante Rosa was carrying out attacks and assassinations against government targets in Italy, and fleeing to Czechoslovakia when they felt threatened by the authorities. Another subversive organization was Pietro Secchia's Communist paramilitary group, which was strong and professional enough in 1948 to seize control of some sections of northern Italy and assume control of the national telephone network. When Secchia's group disintegrated in 1953, he and many of his followers fled to the Czech capital of Prague. In the late 1960s, Soviet Military Intelligence (GRU) began operating a training course for foreign terrorists in Czechoslovakia, whose graduates included many of the early leaders of the Italian Red Brigades. The founder of the Red Brigades was Carlo Curcio, who also traveled repeatedly to Prague, where he conferred with veterans of the Secchia group. Similarly, the Italian publisher-terrorist Giangiacomo Feltrinelli, another graduate of the GRU course, traveled to Czechoslovakia twenty-two times between 1969 and 1971, finally defecting with the assistance of the Czech security services. Another Italian extremist group, the Nazi-Maoists, was also apparently a concoction of the Czech intelligence services. Additional assistance and training were later given the Red Brigades by the Bulgarian intelligence services, while Sardinian and Sicilian terrorists, as well as Italian neo-Nazi organizations such as Ordine Nero, began receiving training, money, and weapons from the Soviet's new Libyan ally, Muammar Qaddafi.[2]

By the 1960s, the Soviets had established recruitment centers for terrorists of both Marxist and non-Marxist varieties in Moscow—Communist Party members at the Lenin Institute and the non-Marxists at the Patrice Lumumba People's Friendship University. There "students" were selected for training in a network of training camps in Odessa, Baku, Simferopol, and Tashkent, where they were taught propaganda, bomb making, urban warfare, and assassination techniques. The graduates of such courses were often sent to Cuba, Bulgaria, and North Korea. One of the best-known among them was the notorious archterrorist Ramírez Sánchez, known as "Carlos the Jackal." Carlos had been recruited by the KGB in his native Venezuela and educated in the 1960s both in Cuba and at Patrice Lumumba in Moscow before embarking on one of the most publicized terror sprees of the century, including the takeover of an OPEC ministers' gathering in Vienna in 1975 and a murderous attack on a French police train in 1982.[3] (When international terrorism could no longer be pursued on this footing, Carlos had outlived his usefulness, and apparently found a place of refuge in Syria—until he was packed off to the Sudan in 1994 and from there deported to France, apparently sacrificed as a gambit by Syria in order to curry favor with the West.)

The willingness to engage in terror, albeit under the control and supervision of the Party hierarchy in Moscow, was always part of Soviet Communist internationalism. Support for the construction of the international terrorist infrastructure was provided by the International Department of the Central Committee of the Communist Party, the Soviet Security Police (KGB), and Soviet Military Intelligence (GRU).[4] But the centrality of terrorism to Soviet foreign policy emerged only in the 1960s, with the stalemate in the Cold War and the emergence of independent Arab states willing to hitch their oil revenues and their war against Israel to the terrorist internationale. During the 1950s, it still appeared as though containment might fail, and the Communist juggernaut would continue its expansion into Southeast Asia, southern Europe, Africa, the Middle East, and South America. But by the 1960s, the nuclear balance of terror between the superpowers had cooled any lingering Soviet interest in open confrontations with the West. The borders of the conflict had more or less stabilized. The Soviet Union was shut out of any substantial influence in the democratic countries, and the Cold War had devolved into a series of proxy confrontations in the Third World. Since a direct assault on the democracies had become unthinkable, the Soviets developed international terror as one of the weapons in their arsenal for carrying on the Communist struggle in many Western strongholds, while maintaining plausible deniability about their complicity.

Here the carefully concealed, one-step-removed brand of Soviet-supported terrorism found a ready partner in the rabid anti-Western antipathies of the radical Arab regimes led by Syria, Libya, and Iraq. Most of these countries were established in mid-century, and they fulminated with rage over what they considered to be centuries of Western oppression of a humiliated Arab world. Even less able than the Soviets to take on the West directly, these Arab regimes embarked on a covert terrorist campaign against American and Western targets, though they showed little of the aptitude and finesse of the Soviets in covering their tracks. Terror, of course, had been a staple crop of Middle Eastern politics for a thousand years, since the time of the eleventh-century Shiite Assassin sect, originally called *hashishin,* for the hashish with which they drugged themselves to better carry out their deadly attacks against their Seljuk Turkish rulers. But it was only with the emergence of independent Arab states that this tested weapon of subduing opponents was transformed into a habitual tool of foreign policy, rivaling oil as the Middle East's chief export, and reaching practically every part of the world.

State-sponsored terror of a more limited variety had in fact been a constant factor in the Arab war against Israel. The Jewish communities in mandatory Palestine were subjected to campaigns of terror from the 1920s on. After Israel's independence in 1948, Egypt and Syria continued to encourage cross-border *fedayeen* attacks, which claimed hundreds of lives and resulted in Israeli counteractions on the Arab side of its borders. In 1964 and 1965, Egypt and Syria established rival "Palestine Liberation" groups modeled after the National Liberation Front (FLN), whose eight-year insurgent war had succeeded in driving the French from Algeria only two years earlier. The avowed goal of both of these organizations was the "liberation of Palestine," which in practice meant liberating it from both the Israeli and the Jordanian states. The Egyptian group, called the Palestine Liberation Organization, was led by Ahmed Shukeiri, whom the diplomat and historian Conor Cruise O'Brien later referred to as a "windbag's windbag." More deadly was the Fatah organization sponsored by Syria and headed by Yasir Arafat, which by 1967 had mounted a campaign of cross-border attacks primarily against Israeli civilian targets. After the defeat of the Arab armies in the Six-Day War of that year, Arafat dumped Shukeiri and became the head of a unified PLO structure.

Early on, Arafat recognized that the support of various Arab states would be insufficient to produce any kind of sustained terrorist campaign against Israel. Egyptian President Nasser's fulminations notwithstanding, Shukeiri had never been permitted to launch extensive attacks from Egyptian soil for fear of triggering an unplanned Israeli response; Arafat himself had been kept on a short leash in Syria, and his gunmen had run into trouble with Jordanian troops from the very first. (In September 1970, King Hussein expelled the PLO from Jordan in a bloody stroke that left ten thousand dead.) Arafat therefore intensified PLO ties with the Soviet bloc, which would help him wage an unrelenting terrorist war against Israel. One of his first encounters was with Fidel Castro, who had repeatedly welcomed him to Havana from 1965 on. Later, the Soviets trained thousands of PLO operatives, awarded them special diplomatic status, and allowed them free movement throughout the countries of the Eastern bloc.[5]

By the early 1970s, Arafat had established a quasi-independent PLO state in southern Lebanon. The Lebanese government was too weak to extend its authority into the south of the country, and within this domain Arafat was able to set up shop, creating a mini-state which enjoyed a close relationship with the Soviet Union and its satellites. This quasi-independent base was to be the propelling force behind the tidal wave of international terror which hit the Western democracies in the two decades that followed.

As noted, the Soviets had supported terrorist insurgents since World War II, but had carefully avoided taking direct responsibility for launching terrorist campaigns against the NATO powers. Other states were in some cases willing to take the heat in exchange for Soviet support in other areas; Libya and North Korea, for example, covered for the Soviets by providing a place of refuge for airline hijackers, allowing the Soviets to insist that they were opposed to this particular type of terror. But Arafat offered what no other nation in the world was willing to provide. Receiving generous Eastern bloc support, he established in Lebanon a training center and launching ground for international terrorism the world over. The Soviets could merely deny knowledge of what was taking place, and the various branches of the PLO would happily collude in a worldwide movement of terror against the Western countries. Like Lenin before him observing the destabilization of czarist Russia at the hands of the SR, Brezhnev could benefit from the destabilization of the capitalist societies under pressure of the terrorist weapon, while being able to keep his hands relatively clean.

Within short order, the Soviet–PLO axis had managed to transform an astonishing collection of domestic terrorist factions into a full-blown international movement devoted to anti-Western and anti-Israeli political violence. In time, the PLO's newfound playground of horrors offered a base of operations and a safe haven for virtually every one of the most notorious terror groups ever to raise its head. The IRA, the German Baader-Meinhof, the Red Army Faction, and numerous neo-Nazi splinters, the Italian Red Brigades, the Japanese Red Army, the French Action Directe, the Sandinistas and a dozen other Latin American groups, the Turkish Liberation Army, the Armenian Asala, the Kurdish PKK, and the Iranian Revolutionary Guards—all came to the PLO camps in Lebanon, were trained and armed there, and were dispatched to their targets. In 1972, the alliance was formalized at a terrorist conference organized in Badawi, Lebanon, by George Habash, head of the Popular Front for the Liberation of Palestine (PFLP) faction of the PLO. At the end of the Badawi Conference, Habash triumphantly announced: "We have created organic supports between the Palestinians and the revolutionaries of the entire world." The nature of these "organic supports" became obvious as the PLO's "Black September" group (operated by Abu Iyad of Arafat's Fatah faction) carried out firebombings in Trieste for the Red Brigades; Japanese Red Army gunmen massacred pilgrims in Israel's Ben-Gurion airport; Italian terrorists were caught smuggling Soviet-made SAM-7 missiles for the PFLP; German terrorists participated with Palestinian gunmen in the Entebbe hijacking; and the Palestinian Liberation Front (PLF) carried out joint attacks on Israeli and Jewish targets in Europe with Odfried Hepp's VSBD neo-Nazi group.[6]

Arafat's activities in Lebanon were replicated to different degrees by Libya, Syria, Iraq, and South Yemen. They cut deals with dozens of terror factions, allowing them to establish head offices in their respective capitals, providing them with training, diplomatic cover, financing, and refuge in exchange for terrorist services directed at enemies of their choice. These states soon became a second, independent source of international terror. Essentially radical Pan-Arabists in their ideologies—the ideas of Libya's Muammar Qaddafi being an original cross between Pan-Arab fascism and militant Islam—their great enemy was and is the West, which they understood to have dismembered the Arab world and left it "colonized" by pro-Western lackeys such as the Saudi and Kuwaiti royal families. Each of the regimes made its own independent arrangements with the Soviets, enjoying Soviet military assistance and diplomatic support, in exchange for its staunch anti-Western stance. Libya in particular became a clearinghouse for Soviet military equipment. In 1976, it was party to one of the largest arms deals in history, purchasing perhaps $12 billion worth of arms, a small part of which were in turn supplied to terrorist groups around the world, including the PLO, the IRA, Carlos's Arm of the Arab Revolution group, the Baader-Meinhof, the Japanese Red Army, and other terrorist and insurgent groups in Turkey, Iran, Yemen, Eritrea, Chad, Chile, Uruguay, Nicaragua, and the Philippines.[7]

The full extent of the Soviet-Arab terrorist network—indeed, the fact that it *was* a network—was throughout the traumatic years of international terrorism obscured by successful efforts to "delegate" much of the violence to other Eastern bloc and Arab regimes that could be blamed for these activities. For example, much of Soviet covert operations in the Western Hemisphere was taken over by the Cuban secret service, the DGI, although it eventually became clear that the DGI was itself nothing more than an arm of Soviet intelligence. And in all the

Western countries, including the United States, there prevailed the view that the incredible wave of terrorism gripping the Western countries was indeed the work of frustrated and deranged individuals, or else groups responding to local problems resulting from oppression of one sort or another. It was not until 1982, when Israel invaded the PLO's labyrinth of training bases in southern Lebanon, that extensive documentation was captured giving an idea of the actual magnitude of the international cooperation between the terrorist groups and the supportive climate that had been afforded them by their sponsors.

The Israeli incursion resulted in the destruction of the kingdom of terror that the PLO had carefully built up in south Lebanon over more than a decade. The leadership of the PLO was expelled to Tunis, where its ability to wreak havoc was significantly curtailed. Moreover, the mid-1980s saw the West open up a broad and unprecedented offensive against international terror. This offensive was first and foremost political; it was intended to expose those countries supporting terror, and to unequivocally label terrorism as immoral, regardless of the identity of the terrorists and their professed motives.

The political offensive had been preceded by a deliberate intellectual effort spanning a number of years to persuade the West to change its policies regarding terrorism. It was in the context of these efforts that the Jonathan Institute was founded. Named after my brother Jonathan, who had fallen while leading the Israeli force that rescued the hostages at Entebbe in 1976, its purpose was to educate free societies as to the nature of terrorism and the methods needed to fight it. The Jonathan Institute's first international conference on terrorism, held in Jerusalem in 1979, stipulated that terror had become a form of political warfare waged against the Western democracies by dictatorial regimes. The participants at the conference, among them Senator Henry Jackson and George Bush, then a candidate for the U.S. presidency, provided evidence of the direct involvement of the Eastern bloc and Arab regimes in spawning international terror. These revelations met with no small amount of resistance—so much that a correspondent covering the conference for *The Wall Street Journal* commented that "a considerable number in the press corps covering the conference were much annoyed."[8] The idea that terrorism was not merely a random collection of violent acts by desperate individuals but a means of purposeful warfare pursued by states and international organizations was at that time simply too much for many to believe. (After the collapse of the Soviet Union, I had the opportunity to discuss this incredulity with a number of officials of the former Soviet bloc, and they expressed astonishment at the naïveté of Western journalists and government figures in this regard.) Yet these and other revelations had a sobering effect on Soviet sponsorship of terror in the 1980s. Increasingly, the glare of publicity regarding their complicity in terrorism impaired the Soviet Union's capacity to pursue détente, and forced it to back off from supporting terrorist groups—even compelling it to begin denouncing terrorism with fewer and fewer reservations. By mid-decade, Soviet support for international terrorism was almost a thing of the past.

At the second conference of the Jonathan Institute, held in Washington in 1984, the participants, including leading figures in American politics, called for political, economic, and military sanctions against the states sponsoring terrorism. The proceedings were edited by me into a book entitled *Terrorism: How the West Can Win*, to which I contributed an essay arguing the need to take direct military action against the terrorist states, which by then were primarily radical Arab regimes. The essay and other sections of the book were reprinted in *Time* magazine and read by prominent members of the U.S. administration—leading some commentators in the Arab press to pin the "blame" on me for some of the subsequent American actions against terrorist states.

From the beginning of my involvement with the Jonathan Institute, and later in my tenure as a diplomat, I believed that the key to the elimination of international terror was having the United States lead the battle, and that this American leadership would harness the countries of the free world into line, much as a powerful locomotive pulls the cars of a train. But it was no simple matter to change the minds of American opinion makers on this subject. Since the view that prevailed in the United States in the late 1970s and early 1980s held that terrorism was the result of political and social oppression, the inescapable conclusion was that terror could not be eliminated without first bringing these conditions to an end. My colleagues and I rejected this view out of hand.

We believed that the American position was not set in stone and that it could be changed by a vigorous effort to present the truth to the American public. At the heart of this effort was bringing to light basic facts about international terrorism, some of which were publicly unavailable. The evidence was checked and rechecked, and from it emerged a clear picture: International terrorism was the result of collusion between dictatorial states and an international terrorist network—a collusion which had to be fought and could be defeated.

Israel played an important role in persuading the United States to adopt this stance. In the military sphere, Israel served as an example of an uncompromising fight against terrorism. The refusal of successive Israeli governments to capitulate to terrorist demands—a refusal that found expression in the repeated assaults by the Israel Defense Forces against terrorists in hostage situations from Maalot to Entebbe—and the Israeli policy of active military pursuit of terrorists into their strongholds, showed other nations that it was possible to fight terrorism.

On the political level, Israel's representatives in the United States waged a concerted campaign to convince American citizens that they should adopt similar policies. This effort began in full force during Moshe Arens's tenure as ambassador to Washington in 1982. Arens arrived in the United States shortly before the Israeli campaign against the PLO terrorist haven in Lebanon. The United States was hostile to this operation, and the Reagan administration applied various pressures to rein in the assault, including suspending delivery of fighter planes to the Israeli Air Force. Arens did much to reverse the American position, especially through the special relationship he was able to establish with Secretary of State George Shultz and President Ronald Reagan.

In July of that year, I joined the embassy as deputy ambassador and soon participated in the effort to persuade the American government to shift its policy to a more aggressive opposition to terrorism. When Arens returned to Israel in 1983 to serve as Minister of Defense, I served for six months as acting ambassador. During this period I kept up the contacts with Shultz. Both in diplomatic channels and in appearances in the media, I used every opportunity to attack international terrorism and the regimes and organizations that stood behind it. The West could defeat international terrorism, I insisted, provided that it adopt two principles as the foundation stones of its policy. First, it must refuse to yield to terrorist demands; and second, it must be ready to confront the regimes sponsoring terror. I repeatedly called for an active policy that would include diplomatic, economic, and even military sanctions against these states.

One of the early supporters of an active American policy against international terrorism was Secretary of State George Shultz. Shultz was particularly shaken by the series of car bombings in 1983 aimed at the American embassy in Beirut, and the American and French servicemen stationed there as peacekeepers under the agreement negotiated for the PLO withdrawal. The bombings left many hundreds dead, including 240 American Marines. At one point during this terrible year, Shultz called me into his office and told me that he was extremely concerned about the spread of terrorism. "These terrorists aren't human beings," he said. "They're animals."

He made it clear that he was determined to effect a change in American anti-terror policy from one of passive defense to a more active one, taking the battle against the terrorists to their bases abroad and to the countries supporting them, "even if there are some who are opposed to this." (He meant primarily Defense Secretary Caspar Weinberger, who was hesistant about using America's armed forces against terrorist targets.) Shultz suggested a series of meetings in which we could work to define what the United States could do in conjunction with the other countries of the free world to uproot the terrorist scourge. I told him that the Jonathan Institute would be holding a second conference, this time in Washington, and suggested that he speak at the conference and make his position clear.

On July 4, 1984, seven years after the Entebbe rescue, Shultz made the following statement to the gathered diplomats and journalists at the conference:

Many countries have joined the ranks of what we might call the "League of Terror" as full-fledged sponsors and supporters of indiscriminate, and not so indiscriminate, murder ... The epidemic is spreading, and the civilized world is still groping for remedies.

Nevertheless, there is also cause for hope. Thanks

in large measure to the efforts of concerned governments and private organizations like the Jonathan Institute, the peoples of the free world have finally begun to grapple with the problem of terrorism, in intellectual and in practical terms...

What we have learned about terrorism is, first, that it is not random, undirected, purposeless violence. It is not, like an earthquake or a hurricane, an act of nature before which we are helpless. Terrorists and those who support them have definite goals; terrorist violence is the means of attaining those goals... With rare exceptions, they are trying to impose their will by force, a special kind of force designated to create an atmosphere of fear. And their efforts are directed at destroying what we are seeking to build...

Can we as a country, can the community of free nations, stand in a purely defensive posture and absorb the blows dealt by terrorists? I think not. From a practical standpoint, a purely passive defense does not provide enough of a deterrent to terrorism and the states that sponsor it. It is time to think long, hard, and seriously about more active means of defense—defense through appropriate preventive or preemptive actions against terrorist groups *before* they strike.[9]

Shultz was as good as his word. He and President Ronald Reagan took the lead in mounting an unprecedented war against international terrorism. Under their leadership, the United States imposed diplomatic and economic sanctions against terrorist states such as Libya, Syria, and Iran. They fought with determination to apprehend the PLO gunmen who murdered a wheelchair-bound American named Leon Klinghoffer aboard the hijacked cruise ship *Achille Lauro* in 1985—to the point of intercepting the terrorists' escape plane in midair over the Mediterranean. Above all, they sent a powerful message to terrorists the world over when, together with Margaret Thatcher's Britain, they bombed Libya, in a raid in which Qaddafi himself nearly lost his life.

Later that year, a TWA airliner was hijacked by Arab gunmen to Beirut, where the passengers were held as hostages. In order to sharpen their demand for the release of terrorists jailed in Kuwait and Lebanese Shiites being held by Israel, the gunmen murdered an American passenger in cold blood and threw his body on the tarmac. Fearing that American troops would storm the plane, the terrorists subsequently scattered the hostages among safehouses in various parts of Beirut, in effect eliminating the option of an Entebbe-style rescue. At the start of the crisis, a special communications channel was established between Shultz and the two key leaders in the government of Israel, Prime Minister Shimon Peres and Foreign Minister Yitzhak Shamir (who, although of opposing parties, were jointly ruling in a National Unity Government); I was then serving as Israel's ambassador to the United Nations, and sensitive messages concerning the crisis were passed back and forth through my office. Shultz's assistant Charlie Hill called me daily to brief the

Israeli government on developments and consult with us as to how the United States should proceed. Even during the first stage of the crisis, I had insisted that the key to escaping from the trap would be an unequivocal American refusal to give in to the demands of the terrorists under any circumstance. But when the hostages were dispersed throughout Beirut, the terrorists escalated their demands, threatening to begin killing the hostages immediately if these demands were not met. The day this ultimatum was issued, Hill called me to ask what I thought the American response should be.

"Issue a counter-threat," I told him. "Make it clear to the terrorists that if they so much as touch a hair on any of the hostages' heads, you won't rest until every last one of them has been hunted down and wiped out."

Hill said he would pass the message to Shultz. Days later, he called back to say that they had acted on this recommendation and that the results had been positive. Over the following days, the Americans were unrelenting in their firm and uncompromising posture. The terrorists eventually tempered their demands, and the tension began to subside. At the height of the crisis, the Israeli government had offered to release the Shiite prisoners in its custody—but according to the original timetable which had been set before the hijacking. Shultz had objected to this offer, because it sounded like a partial acceptance of the terrorists' conditions. A few weeks later, a face-saving compromise was arranged, whereby the hostages were released, followed by the release of Israeli-held Shiite prisoners according to the original timetable.

The central demand—the release of the terrorists' comrades in Kuwait—was not met.

These successes encouraged the Reagan administration to work for an overall change in the Western stance toward terrorism. In 1986, the United States called a summit conference of Western leaders in Tokyo, in which sweeping resolutions were adopted calling for an aggressive Western defense against international terrorism. And in 1987, Congress passed the firmest anti-terrorist legislation yet, ordering the closure of all PLO offices in the United States. The law stated that "the PLO is a terrorist organization, which threatens the interests of the United States and its allies."

After twenty years in which international terrorism under the leadership of the PLO had enjoyed virtually unrestricted freedom of action, the West had finally begun to grasp the principle that the terrorist organizations and their state sponsors should no longer be able to escape punishment for their deeds. The growing understanding of the nature of terrorist methods, combined with the very real threat of further American operations against terrorist bases and terrorist states around the world, undermined the foundations on which international terror had been built.

Of course, the West's battle against terrorism was not without its setbacks. The worst of these was the revelation in November 1986 that even as the United States had been stepping up its war against terrorism, elements in the Reagan White House had been simultaneously negotiating with Iranian-controlled terrorists in Lebanon for the release of American hostages in their custody. The agreed-upon price was shipments of American weapons to the regime in Iran. The media reported that three shipments had been sent—one for each hostage released—but that the terrorists, knowing a good deal when they saw one, had during the same period taken three new hostages. As the news of the American capitulation broke, Secretary of State Shultz told his assistant: "After years of work, the keystone of our counterterrorism policy was set: No deals with terrorists. Now we have fallen into the trap. We have voluntarily made ourselves the victims of the terrorist extortion racket. We have spawned a hostage-taking industry. Every principle that the President praised in Netanyahu's book on terrorism has been dealt a terrible blow by what has been done."[10] (He was referring to *Terrorism: How the West Can Win*, which, according to Shultz, President Reagan had read on the way to the Tokyo summit on terrorism.) Fortunately, Shultz's tenacious campaign to steer the United States away from its dealings with Iran paid off. Within a matter of weeks, he was able to reassert control over Middle East policy, and the American government returned to the original course he had set with President Reagan.

Despite the setbacks, the Reagan–Shultz anti-terror policy of the 1980s was an immense overall success. International terrorism was dealt a stunning defeat. Its dictatorial affiliations were laid bare, its perpetrators unmasked. The sharp political, economic, and military blows delivered by the West against its chief sponsors caused them to rescind their support and rein in the terrorists. And the destruction of the PLO base in Lebanon deprived the Soviets and the Arab world of their most useful staging ground for terrorist operations against the democracies. The Soviet–Arab terrorist axis was on the verge of extinction. The West's airlines, cities, and citizens seemed to be safe once again. After nearly twenty years of being subjected to continual savagery, the entire scaffolding of international terrorism appeared to have collapsed into the dust.

IV

The 1990s: The Rise of
Militant Islam in America
and the World

O_r had it?

As with any form of aggression, deterring terrorist violence requires constant vigilance. There is no one-step solution available in which the democracies take forceful action against the sources of terror and then proceed to forget about the problem. For the problem as such will not go away. Terrorism is rooted in the deepest nature of the dictatorial regimes and organizations that practice it. That they are prone to violent coercion, including terror, is not an incidental characteristic of dictatorships; it is their quintessential, defining attribute. And as long as they retain their dictatorial nature, they will retain their proclivity for terror. Unless constantly checked and suppressed, this tendency will manifest itself again and again. Of course, when a regime like Soviet Communism is replaced by a democratically elected government, this has an immediate effect. Post-Communist Russia is no longer in the business of supporting international terror, and no action is required to ensure that this remains the case. But barring such a dramatic revolution in political philosophy and policy, the basic inclination toward terrorism remains deeply embedded in its chief practitioners and sponsors, and they must be constantly reminded that they will pay dearly for such conduct if they practice it against other societies.

Yet it is precisely this message, potently delivered by the United States and its allies in the second half of the 1980s, that has been obscured and enfeebled in the 1990s. After their impressive victories, some of the Western security services quickly relaxed their anti-terror posture in the pursuit of terrorist cells on their home turf. For example, in Germany the authorities let up the pressure on neo-Nazi groups, with the result that they began to have a renaissance of sorts. Equally, the all-out effort to deter naked aggression in the Gulf War convinced some in the West that they had resolutely defused the potential for aggression from the Middle East. But this was not the case. The results of the Gulf War were hardly decisive in discouraging terror from the Middle East.

First, while the conquest of Kuwait by Iraq was a clear act of aggression for the entire world to see (and punish), terrorism is invariably secretive, relying on its deniability for impunity. The deterrent effect that applies to aggression carried out in broad daylight does not necessarily apply to aggression carried out in the dark.

Second, that very deterrent effect with regard to Iraq was itself eroded by the inconclusive end of the Gulf War. The punishment meted out to Saddam Hussein was not, as it transpires, that severe after all; a monumental American blunder at the end of an otherwise brilliantly executed war left the fifty-one-year-old tyrant in power in Iraq, sparing him to rise and possibly fight another day.

Third, Iraq's enemy to the east, Iran, a terrorist state par excellence, paid no price whatsoever in the Gulf War and was even accorded considerable legitimacy as a tacit ally.

Fourth, Iraq's enemy to the west, Syria, another classic terrorist state, also benefited enormously from the war. For the privilege of seeing its archenemy Iraq crushed by the West, it received badly needed economic assistance, and was offered great respectability in the attainment of its strategic objectives, such as pushing Israel off the Golan Heights and digesting what remained of Lebanon. Since the Madrid Peace Conference convened by the United States and Russia after the war, the Western countries have seldom, if ever, demanded that Syria clearly cease its sponsorship of terror or that it dismantle the headquarters of the dozen terrorist movements based in Damascus, lest such "upsetting" efforts drive the Syrian dictator, Hafez Assad, away from the Western orbit.

Fifth, after the Gulf War, a new base was added to the roster of terrorist havens in the form of PLO-controlled Gaza, which quickly became a safe haven for several Islamic terrorist movements.

The result of all this was that by the mid-1990s international terrorism's major Middle Eastern sponsors were far from defeated and prostrate. Some of them got up, dusted themselves off, and were ready to resume their former practices, admittedly with greater caution and concealment this time. Most important, they were joined by new bullies on the block. Undoubtedly the most important new forces propelling international terrorism in the 1990s have been the Islamic Republic of Iran and the militant Sunni Islamic movements that have assumed an international character. Already active in the 1980s, these forces have escalated their activities in recent years, providing the spiritual and material wellspring of an ever-growing gallery of Islamic terrorist groups. Most prominent is the Iranian Revolutionary Guards, who rose to prominence in the Khomeinist Shiite revolution in Iran in 1979 and soon afterward sent expeditionary forces to Lebanon. Once in Lebanon, they were instrumental in spawning the Shiite terror organization Hizballah, the Party of God, which with Syrian and Iranian sponsorship masterminded the terrorist attacks that drove the American forces out of the country in the mid-1980s. Hizballah is presently the major terrorist force in south Lebanon, launching incessant attacks against Israel's northern border. It is suspected of involvement in a number of bombing attacks around the world, including the 1988 midair destruction of a Pan Am airliner over Lockerbie, Scotland, which claimed 258 lives, and the 1994 bombing of the Jewish community building in Buenos Aires, which left nearly a hundred dead and hundreds more wounded.

Together, the Iranians and Hizballah have begun nurturing additional affiliate groups such as the Palestinian Islamic Jihad, which operates against Israel, and similar groups active in other countries.

Iran, Hizballah, and their satellite organizations have rapidly replaced both Communism and Pan-Arab fascism as the driving force behind international terror. For years after the Iranian revolution, the potential of this force was suppressed by the interminable Iran-Iraq war, which began when the militant Iranian regime had barely come to power. But by 1989, this war came to an end, allowing Iran a breathing space in which to flex its international muscles in new directions and try its hand at a new kind of militant Islamic diplomacy. A hint of the potential power of this policy was provided by the convening of a special Islamic conference called by Iran and held in Teheran in October 1991, on the eve of the Madrid Peace Conference between Israel and its Arab neighbors; the Teheran conference was attended by radical Islamic movements and terrorist groups from forty countries, and declared itself to be against making any kind of peace with the Jewish state. While Libya and Iraq have chafed under the yoke of Western sanctions (imposed on Libya in 1986 in the wake of its complicity in the bombing of a discotheque in Germany frequented by American servicemen, and on Iraq in 1991 after its invasion of Kuwait), and while the other Pan-Arabist state, Syria, has had to tone down its more overt associations with international terrorism to win U.S. pressure on Israel, Iran has gone virtually unscathed, carefully cultivating a modern international terrorist network of which the Soviets would have been proud.

But while many people are aware of this Iranian practice, few have yet recognized that the Iranian-sponsored terrorist web is not the only source of militant Islamic terror. After all, the Iranians are mainly Shiites, and they therefore do not command the automatic attention and allegiance of Sunni militants, who stem from the other great branch of Islam. Yet one event served to activate this hitherto dormant Sunni potential for violence. The Soviet invasion of Afghanistan in 1979 resulted in a dramatic inpouring of volunteers into the ranks of the Afghani *Mujahdeen* fighting the Soviet occupation, a *Who's Who* of zealots from throughout the world of Sunni Islam. Funded by the United States and Saudi Arabia— the Americans alone poured in $3 billion—the war in Afghanistan became to Sunni Islam what the Spanish Civil War was to the Communists; it created an international brotherhood of fighting men, well versed in the ways of terrorism. And while the Islamic resistance during the Afghan war was more similar to the Unita insurgents in Angola than it was to the world of Arab terrorism, times have changed. The Soviet Union completed its withdrawal from Kabul in 1989, and the Islamic resistance forces have since dispersed. Unlike the volunteers in the war against Franco, the Islamic resistance won, offering proof of the innate faithful supremacy of Islam over the infidel powers. In many cases these providential warriors have since been in search of the next step on the road to the triumph of Islam. Often they have had to move from country to country, having been denied the right to return to their home countries for fear that their excessive zeal would find an outlet there. Since the end of the war in Afghanistan, an international Sunni terrorist network has thus sprung into being, composed in the main of Islamic veterans and their religious leaders. It has built a sympathetic relationship with the government of Sudan and has excellent ties with the fundamentalist side in the simmering civil war in Algeria, the Muslim Brotherhood in Egypt, the Hamas terrorists of Gaza, and the increasingly influential militant Islamicists in Tunisia, Pakistan, and Indonesia. It is this group which is associated with bombers of the World Trade Center in Manhattan. And if it succeeds in its strategic goal of toppling the present Egyptian government, it will have harnessed the most powerful country in the Arab world in the service of the new Islamic terror. On June 26, 1995, this horrible possibility might have become a reality as gunmen opened fire on Egyptian President Hosni Mubarak's motorcade as it made its way through the Ethiopian capital of Addis Ababa. According to Egyptian sources, a villa by the roadside had been rented by Sudanese nationals, and accusations were leveled at Hassan Tourabi's militant Islamic group based in the Sudan. Following the abortive attack, tensions flared between the Sudan and Egypt, and both countries amassed troops on their common border. Whatever the true identity of the masterminds, the implications of the attack are clear: The new Sunni militancy is growing bolder, and the old Arab order is running for cover.

It is impossible to understand just how inimical—and how deadly—to the United States and to Europe this rising tide of militant Islam is without taking a look at the roots of Arab-Islamic hatred of the West. Because of the Western media's fascination with Israel, many today are under the impression that the intense hostility prevalent in the Arab and Islamic world toward the United States is a contemporary phenomenon, the result of Western support for the Jewish state, and that such hostility would end if an Arab–Israeli peace was eventually reached. But nothing could be more removed from the truth. The enmity toward the West goes back many centuries, remaining to this day a driving force at the core of militant Arab-Islamic political culture. And this would have been the case even if Israel had never been born.

To fully appreciate the enduring hatred of the West by today's Islamic militants, it is necessary to understand the historic roots of this enmity. Few Westerners are familiar with even the highlights of the strained history of relations between Islam and the West, a history which is the cornerstone of Islamic education throughout the entire Arab world—how in the year 630 the Arab prophet Muhammad united the Arab peoples, forging them into a nation with a fighting religion whose destiny was to bring the word of Allah and the rule of Islam to all mankind. Within a century, Muhammad and his followers had made the Muslim Arabs the rulers of a vast empire, conquering the Middle East, Persia, India and the Asian interior, North Africa, Asia Minor, and Spain, and lunging deep into France. Had it not been for Charles

Martel, who in 732 defeated the Arabs at Poitiers, 180 miles south of Paris, Europe might have been an Islamic continent today—a fact that Arab political culture has never forgotten. Indeed, for 950 years after that defeat, much of Islamic history focused on the struggle to prevent the reconquest of Muslim lands by the Christians, particularly the Holy Land, Spain, and southern Italy, and the longing for a great leader, the caliph, who would set right the historic wrong, resurrecting the glory of Islam by finally achieving the defeat of European power. This was a dream powerful enough to bring the armies of the Ottoman sultan to the gates of Vienna, where the Muslim thrust into Europe was broken in 1683.

The subsequent decline of Ottoman power relative to the Christian powers, particularly Britain and France, was long and painful. By 1798, Napoleon was in command of a modern citizen-army which was able to seize Egypt without difficulty. By the 1830s, Algeria had become a permanent French base and the British had seized control of ports along the Arabian coast. Within fifty years, all of North Africa and much of the Persian Gulf had become British, French, and Italian possessions. And in 1914, with the beginning of World War I, the final dismantling of what was left of the realm of Islam began. In the aftermath of World War I, Turkey was established as a Western-style secular state, and the Arab world was put under European control: Morocco, Algeria, and Syria under France; Egypt, Arabia, and Iraq under Britain. Iran, too, was placed under the control of a pro-Western royal family in the 1930s. After a tortuous history of fourteen centuries, which had seen triumph and decline, the political independence of the Islamic world appeared to come to a final and complete end.

There can be no exaggerating the confusion and humiliation which descended on the Arab and Muslim world as a result of these developments. The European powers divided up the map of the former Ottoman lands into several arbitrary entities, and ruled by making alliances with local clans who found the relationship profitable, styling themselves "royal families" and adopting the titles of "king" and "prince" after the European fashion. Many grew wealthy off their special status, some immeasurably so after the great oil discoveries in the 1920s and 1930s. The ruling classes sent their children to study at European universities and gladly assisted in maintaining foreign influence over their economies. Not surprisingly, the result was bitterness and consternation in Arab society, as expressed by a leading Egyptian intellectual: "Anyone who reflects on the present state of the Islamic nation finds it in great calamity. Practically, changing circumstances have forced it to adopt new laws taken directly from foreign codes . . . to arrest its ancient [religious] legislation . . . The nation is tormented and resentful, plagued by inner contradictions and fragmentation, its reality is contrary to its ideals and its comportment goes against its creed. What a horrible state for a nation to live in."[1]

Not long after the establishment of the European protectorates throughout the Arab world, two streams of thought emerged to challenge the "horrible state" in which the Muslim Arabs found themselves. The first, the Pan-Arab nationalism of Egypt's Nasser and the Baath Party in Syria and Iraq, was consciously modeled after the Pan-German nationalism which had succeeded in unifying the fragmented German people in the nineteenth century and had resurrected a defeated Germany between the two world wars. Pan-Arabism actively supported Hitler's "achievements" in Europe and collaborated with him against the British in the Middle East during the war. An ideology tailor-made for Arab military men, it dreamed of the creation of a modern and unified Arab-fascist nation. The second stream was that of the Muslim Brotherhood and other Islamic fundamentalist organizations, which rejected Pan-Arabism as yet another alien ideological strain, regarding its proponents as heretics. The Islamicists claimed to be returning to the true roots of Muslim Arab greatness by advocating the unification of all the Arab realms under a "pure" Islamic regime.

What the two movements had in common was their abiding hatred of the weakness and treachery of the Arab monarchies (and of the Shah's rule in Iran) and of the Western powers, which they believed to have dismembered the Islamic world, leaving it humiliated, impoverished, divided, and culturally colonized. As soon as the Arab states began to achieve full independence after World War II, these two movements began working to dispose of the Arab monarchs, with no small measure of success: Three decades later, the pro-Western monarchs of Egypt, Iraq, and Libya had been deposed and replaced

by Pan-Arabist military regimes of one stripe or another—all of them eager to devote themselves to the task
of dismantling the remaining Arab monarchies and add-
ing them to their own realms; all of them sympathetic
to the confrontation with the West being spearheaded by
the Soviet Union; all of them recognizing the liberation
of Jerusalem as a central vehicle for stirring up ultra-
nationalist sentiment among their people; and all of them
possessing no hesitation about resorting to terrorism to
achieve these ends. As Egyptian President Nasser, the
leading proponent of Pan-Arab nationalism, said on the
eve of the Six-Day War: "We are confronting Israel and
the West as well—the West, which created Israel and
despised us Arabs, and which ignored us before and after
1948. They had no regard for our feelings, our hopes in
life, our rights . . . If the Western powers disavow our
rights and ridicule and despise us, we Arabs must teach
them to respect us and take us seriously."[2] It was this
school of thought, too, which produced Yasir Arafat's
PLO, whose "Palestine National Covenant"—which to
this date has not been officially canceled by its constitutional author, the Palestine National Council—is a
hodgepodge of Nasserist Pan-Arab fascism and Marxist
clichés about the end of "colonialism," all of it aimed at
destroying Israel as a Western intrusion into the Arab
realm.

After years of Arab propaganda directed at the West,
it has become fairly easy to sell the assertion of Western
Arabists that if only Israel had not come into being, the
Muslim and Arab relationship with the West would be

harmonious. But in fact, the antagonism of the Islamic world toward the West raged for a millennium before Israel was added to its list of enemies. *The soldiers of militant Islam and Pan-Arabism do not hate the West because of Israel; they hate Israel because of the West.*

From virtually the beginning of the contemporary Jewish resettlement in the land of Israel, parts of the Arab world saw Zionism as an expression and representation of Western civilization, an alien implantation that split the realm of Islam down the middle. Indeed, a common refrain in Arab and Iranian propaganda has it that the Zionists are nothing more than neo-Crusaders; it is only a question of time before the Muslims unite under a latter-day Saladin who will expel this modern "Crusader state" into the sea. That in this larger anti-Western context, militant Arabs understand Israel as a mere tool of the West to be used against them can be seen in the constant references made by Saddam, Assad, and Arafat to Saladin—the great Muslim general who liberated Jerusalem from the European Crusaders in 1187, after having signed a treaty avowing peace. As Arafat recently said, "The PLO offers not the peace of the weak but the peace of Saladin."[3] What is not stated explicitly, but what Muslim audiences understand well in its historical context, is that Saladin's peace treaty with the Crusaders was merely a tactical ruse that was followed by Muslim attacks which wiped out the Christian presence in the Holy Land.[4]

Until recently, then, the dominant anti-Western ideology emanating from the Middle East was Pan-

Arabism, rooted in an abiding hatred of the West, and of Israel as its principal local manifestation. Yet in recent years, when no new Saladin emerged to unify Arabdom, this ideology has waned, only to flare up again briefly when it was thought that Saddam Hussein was ready to play the part of the Great Redeemer. But when Saddam was ignominiously booted out of the veritable Western protectorate of Kuwait, it became demonstrably clear that Pan-Arabism was no match for the hated West. A new force would now vie for the allegiance of those Arabs and Muslims who kept alive the smoldering historic resentment of the West. That force was militant Islam. Basing themselves on an extreme and narrow interpretation of the tradition of Islamic scripture, the new Islamic purists interpreted this entire great faith as pivoting around the obligation to wage incessant and unrelenting *jihad*—the Islamic holy war to free the world from the non-Islamic heathen.

Until the fall of the Shah of Iran, the history of Islamic radicalism was one of agitating against the Pan-Arabist strongmen ruling their countries. Periodically, they would succeed in inflicting a painful blow, as when they assassinated Egyptian President Anwar Sadat in 1981; or in provoking a vicious reprisal, as when Syrian President Hafez Assad leveled the fundamentalist stronghold of Hama, leaving tens of thousands dead, after an abortive uprising there in 1982. These activities gained the militants no operational capacity which could be directed against Israel or the West. Nonetheless they justified directing their terrorist efforts against their own governments by arguing that the *jihad* had to be waged against the enemy closest to home—in this case the secular Arab rulers. Yet with the Iranian revolution in 1979, monies and logistical support for the first time began to be available for more ambitious Islamic terrorist operations outside the Middle East. While the Pan-Arabist regimes had been painfully punished by the West for their aggression—from the American–British bombing of Libya to the allied war effort against Iraq—the flourishing culture of Islamic terrorism in Iran, Sudan, Lebanon, and Gaza has gone virtually untouched by Western anti-terrorist policies, even as it has spread outward and westward: first against foreigners in Lebanon, then against Israel, later against targets in Europe and South America, and finally against the Great Satan itself, the United States.

The infiltration of Islamic terrorism into Europe was not immediately obvious. Many of the European countries now have rapidly expanding Muslim communities, with sizable Muslim "ghettos" already existing in Berlin, Cologne, Paris, Marseilles, and many other European cities. The German, French, and British Muslim communities number in the millions. Of course, this fact by itself is in no way significant; in no way does Islam itself advocate lawlessness or violence. It is a great religion that has fostered, as in medieval Spain, some of the world's most advanced civilizations. Most of the European Muslims, like their co-religionists in the United States and Israel, are law-abiding citizens or residents who would never dream of participating in terrorist activity or in any other illegal act. But a few of them have come under the sway of a perverse and primitive interpretation of the faith, which moves them to fanaticism and violence. And as the Muslim communities in the West continue to grow, a widening fringe of their membership invariably becomes susceptible to infection by the message of militant Islam. Europe has in this way come to be dotted with centers of militant Islamic activity. By 1995 at least fourteen militant Islamic groups were known to be operating throughout Europe, their active membership reaching into the tens of thousands. Thus, one of the co-conspirators in the World Trade Center bombing was assisted by a formidable yet hitherto unnoticed Islamic group in Denmark. Similarly, authorities in Belgium in 1994 uncovered a large cache of weapons, apparently intended for the Islamic Salvation Front (FIS), which is attempting to overthrow the military government in Algeria. The FIS was one of the first suspects of the July 1995 bombing of a Paris subway purportedly carried out to deter France from further support of the Algerian regime. Regardless of the identity of the perpetrators of this particular attack, France's burgeoning Muslim community affords the FIS and other militant Islamic groups ample room for maneuver in that country. A series of weapons smuggling by Italian Muslims ended in June 1995 with the raid by 1,400 Italian police on mosques and other Islamic cultural centers in Milan, Rome, Florence, and other Italian cities. The arrests included the Islamic spiritual leader of Milan and sixteen other activists, who are to be charged with planning the assassination of Egyptian President Hosni Mubarak during a state visit to Italy, as well as attacks against American and Israeli targets. In addition to weapons and forged documents, the Italian authorities seized records linking some of Italy's central Islamic religious establishments to terrorist attacks throughout the world, including the bombing of the World Trade Center in New York.[5]

Germany, too, has become an epicenter of militant European Islamic activities, not only including organizations affiliated with the Iranian-Shiite and Sunni *Mujahdeen* terrorist networks but also those serving as the base for a *third* militant Islamic terror movement—a fanatical Turkish Islamic terrorism which has found a haven among the two-million-strong Turkish community in Germany. Germany is also the center for Iranian-sponsored European radicalism, with organizations such as the Hamburg Islamic Center serving to circulate conspiracy theories accusing the West of trying to destroy the Islamic world. The Iranians also finance the Union of Islamic Student Associations in Europe (UISA), whose members commit to "defend to the death the Islamic faith and Islamic revolution," distributing Khomeiniist ideological materials and recruiting new sympathizers for radical Islam. Other groups with a substantial organizational base in Germany include the Hizballah and Hamas.

Turkey too has recently experienced a rash of Islamic terrorist attacks, quite apart from its lingering battle with the Syrian-sponsored terrorism of the Kurdish Workers' Party (PKK). Much of this new anti-Turkish terrorism emanates from enclaves of Turkish Islamic radicals based in Germany. Other terrorism originates from still another source, the Arab–Israeli conflict. Istanbul itself has been the site of repeated acts of terrorism against Jewish and Israeli targets, including the Iraqi-backed 1986 grenade and machine-gun attack of the Abu Nidal organization against the crowded Neve Shalom synagogue in Istanbul, in which twenty-one people died. This was followed in 1995 with a grenade attack on Istanbul's Beit El synagogue, which fortunately did not claim any lives because two of the grenades failed to explode. Significantly, this last attack was carried out by Hizballah terrorists who have sought, with Iranian support, to make Turkey into a regular staging area for their activities. Within a span of a few years, they have murdered an Israeli embassy security officer, fired rockets at the car of an Israeli official, attempted to assassinate the head of the Turkish Jewish community, Jacques Kimche, and most recently attempted to assassinate Yehuda Yuram, another leader of that same community.

This violence has been supported by German-based Turkish-European organizations such as the Association of Islamic Societies and Communities (ICCB), whose publication *Mohammed's Nation* calls for the violent overthrow of the Turkish government and brands the Jews as enemies of humanity. The head of the ICCB, Cemaleddin Kaplan, known as "the Khomeini of Cologne," was in 1993 ordered deported by the Aliens Office of the city of Cologne, but restrictions on deportation contained in German federal law have allowed the radical spiritual leader to remain in Germany. An even more powerful organization is the Association for a New World Outlook in Europe (AMGT), the European branch of the Turkish Welfare Party (RP). In March 1994, it won 19 percent of the votes in local elections in Turkey, on a platform calling for the (thus far non-violent) establishment of a Turkish Islamic Republic, opposition to the existence of Israel, and the spread of the rule of Islam to the entire world. AMGT has 400 branches throughout Europe and claims 30,000 members.[6]

Many other examples of Islamic terrorist infiltration of Europe, of both the Shiite and Sunni strains, have largely been ignored in public discourse. Most of the European governments are loath to address the issue and do not do so unless a particularly violent attack takes place. Unlike the battle with their "own" domestic terrorist groups, the uprooting of militant Islamic bases on their soil invariably entails a confrontation with Iran or other important regimes in the Islamic world, something most European leaders prefer to avoid for fear of unpleasant diplomatic and economic consequences. The Islamic terrorist network has for this reason been making rapid inroads into every part of Europe, including Britain, and until recently hardly anyone was paying attention.

The same can be said in large measure about the United States. If America has started to take note of the problem of militant Islamic activities within its borders, this has come about only after particularly spectacular attacks by these groups within the United States itself. In November 1990, an Egyptian immigrant to the United

States named El Sayyid Nosair was arrested and charged with murdering Rabbi Meir Kahane in New York.* The subsequent police investigation discovered forty-seven boxes of papers in his home, mostly in Arabic, that the police assumed were "religious materials" of no relevance to the case. They concluded that Nosair was a lone gunman, and never even considered the possibility of a larger conspiracy. It was only in 1993, after the bombing of the World Trade Center, that police returned to these boxes and found them to contain instructions on how to conduct assassinations and attacks on aircraft, as well as formulas for making bombs. In one notebook, Nosair had written: "We have to thoroughly demoralize the enemies of God . . . by means of destroying and blowing up the towers that constitute the pillars of their civilization, such as the tourist attractions and the high buildings of which they are so proud." It transpired that Nosair was a follower of the militant Egyptian Sheikh Omar Abdel Rahman, who had been involved in the assassination of Egyptian President Anwar Sadat, and had set up shop in New Jersey in 1990, preaching *jihad* against non-Islamic Arab governments, Jews, and the West. Other Rahman minions were quickly arrested for the bombing of the Twin Towers—shortly before they were to begin

*Nosair was actually acquitted by the jury on the murder count, a verdict which the judge, Alvin Schleshinger, called "totally against the weight of the evidence; it was irrational . . . It just made no sense, common or otherwise, to have reached that verdict." *Jihad in America* (PBS, final script, November 21, 1994; Executive Producer, Steve Emerson, p. 16). Nosair was found guilty of related charges and sent to prison.

a wave of terror which was to include attacks on the Lincoln and Holland Tunnels as well as the United Nations building, and the assassination of prominent Americans. Nosair had been goading them on from his prison cell.

But Nosair and Sheikh Rahman are by no means alone in the business of promoting *jihad* in the United States. In 1994, a pathbreaking piece of investigative journalism, *Jihad in America*, was aired by PBS, weaving together the threads of the quiltwork of Islamic terrorist groups and terrorist sponsors which have sprung up across America since the Iranian revolution. These include arms of the Hamas, Hizballah, Islamic Jihad, and cells of the Sunni *Mujahdeen*, with centers of activity in Brooklyn, New Jersey, Tampa, Chicago, Detroit, Kansas City—and even Oklahoma City. Hiding behind a smoke screen of religious and charitable Islamic groups and small businesses, these organs work in the United States to raise funds, publish incendiary literature, recruit volunteers, issue orders, and lay plans for terrorist missions abroad, and—like the ultra-rightist Patriot movement—train in the use of automatic weapons in preparation for the ultimate battle against the government of the United States. In recent years the United States has played host to at least a dozen known conferences of international Islamic terrorism, where the Islamic militants coordinated their moves and exchanged logistical information. One gathering in Kansas City in 1989, for example, attracted the militant Egyptian Islamic leader Yousef al-Qaradhawi, Tawfiq Mustapha of the Muslim Liberation Party of Jordan,

Abdullah Anas of the Algerian Islamic Salvation Front, Rashid Ghannushi of the Tunisian fundamentalist group Al-Nahdha, and Sheikh Mohammed Siyyam of the Palestinian Hamas. A graduate of one of these conferences was Mohammed Saleh, a Palestinian-American from Chicago who was arrested in Israel in 1993 for financing the purchase of weapons used to murder four people.

In short, elements in the American Muslim community have rapidly developed into the supportive hinterland necessary to serve as at least a partial home base for international terror directed *outward*, at Israel, Egypt, Algeria, Jordan, and other non-Islamic Middle Eastern regimes. Making use of American freedom of speech and religion, of liberal immigration and visitation laws, and of the relative lack of surveillance which they could hardly enjoy in their own countries, these groups have turned the United States into a terrorist haven in its own right. Again, the salient fact is that every one of these subversive or terrorist groups can operate far more freely in the United States than in their home states. While the United States is certainly not a state sponsor of terror, it has nonetheless become an unwitting state incubator of terror.

And it can only be a matter of time before this terror is turned *inward* against the United States, the leader of the hated West and the country responsible in the eyes of militant Muslims for having created Israel and for maintaining the supposedly heretical Arab regimes. Among the great inciters against America has been Abdullah Azzam, one of the religious leaders who transformed the CIA-backed resistance of the Afghani rebels into a successful Islamic *jihad* against the Soviet Union. In 1989 Azzam was the keynote speaker at what was billed as the First Conference of the *Jihad*, held at the Al-Farooq Mosque in Brooklyn. There, he told the audience: "The *jihad,* the fighting, is obligatory on you wherever you can perform it. And just as when you are in America you must fast . . . so, too, you must wage *jihad.* The word *jihad* means fighting only, fighting with the sword." As Sheikh Omar Abdel Rahman, spiritual leader of the World Trade Center bombers, put it: "The obligation of Allah is upon us to wage *jihad* for the sake of Allah . . . We conquer the lands of the infidels and we spread Islam by calling the infidels to Allah, and if they stand in our way, then we wage *jihad* for the sake of Allah." Nor are Rahman, Azzam, and their ilk impressed with the might of the United States, now that they have had the experience of defeating the Soviets. As Azzam told a crowd in Oklahoma City in 1988: "After Afghanistan, nothing is impossible for us anymore. There are no superpowers . . . What matters is the willpower that springs from our religious belief."[7]

Thus, while the United States struggles to deal with the rising threat of domestic terrorism at home, a new tide of international terrorism has arisen, constructing a worldwide network of hate, possessing weapons, money, and safe havens of unprecedented scope. With residence in the United States and even American citizenship, these international terrorists have now become *domestic* terrorists as well, living in America so that they can wage *jihad* against America. As we have seen, a similar process is well underway in Europe. And it is this wholly new *domestic-international terrorism* which the United States and Europe now face and which threatens to assume even more alarming proportions as a result of two recent developments far from their shores.

V

The Gaza Syndrome

One of the most important boosts Islamic terrorism has received since the establishment of the Islamic Republic in Iran has been the creation of the PLO enclave in Gaza in the wake of the 1993 Oslo accords between Israel and the PLO.

How did the deal between Israel and the PLO come about? Shortly after Israel's victory in the Six-Day War in 1967, it had begun to dawn on portions of the Arab world that there was no possibility of destroying the Jewish state by conventional means. That war had pushed Israel's borders from the outskirts of Tel Aviv to the Jordan Valley forty miles to the east, and from the development towns of the Negev to the Suez Canal one hundred miles to the west. A stone wall a thousand meters high in the form of the Judean-Samarian mountains now provided a formidable barrier to Arab invasion from the east, while the sea and the huge Sinai desert to the southwest shielded Israel's populated coastline from any threat in the west. It was no longer feasible for the Arab armies to simply thrust across Israel's borders directly into the heart of the Jewish state, which had before the Six-Day War been a mere nine miles in width at its narrowest point. That Israel was no longer so vulnerable was confirmed in the Yom Kippur surprise attack of 1973, which began with optimal surprise conditions for the Arab armies but quickly brought the Israel Defense Forces to the outskirts of Cairo and Damascus. The recognition that the Arabs would not be able to defeat Israel within its new boundaries gave birth to two competing approaches toward Israel within Arab politics. The first approach maintained that since the Arabs lacked a credible war option against Israel in its present boundaries, they had no choice but to gradually come to terms with Israel's existence, and eventually to make formal peace with it. It was this line of thinking which, for example, led to the gradual reconciliation between Israel and Jordan, and to the eventual signing of a formal peace between them. Yet simultaneously there developed a second approach, which started out from the same premise but reached a dramatically different conclusion: True, its proponents argued, Israel could not be defeated within its present boundaries; therefore, the proper policy would be to *reduce it to its former indefensible frontiers* and proceed to destroy it from there. Those who held this view believed that Israel could be made to return to the pre-1967 borders through a combination of relentless terrorist attacks and diplomatic pressure by the Arab states on the West to demand Israel's withdrawal.

This second school of thought has been championed by the PLO for over twenty years. Indeed, since the PLO formally adopted what it calls the "Phased Plan" at its 1974 Cairo conference, it has consistently been the most outspoken exponent of this view in the Arab world. According to the Phased Plan, the PLO would at first establish its "state of Palestine" on any territory which "would be evacuated by the Zionist enemy." This new Arab state would then align itself with the other "confrontation states" and prepare for the second stage—the eradication of Israel in a renewed onslaught.[1]

Until 1992, all Israeli governments, whether led by the Labor Party or by the Likud, sought to strengthen the first approach in the Arab world while discouraging the second, striving to achieve peace with the Arab states while remaining within the improved defensive borders. Though there were differences as to what territorial concessions Israel might be prepared to make, there was a broad consensus against returning to the pre-1967 lines, which had been so fragile as to have provoked the Six-Day War, and against the establishment of a PLO state next to Israel. The collapse of the Soviet Union, the chief patron of the Arab dictatorships, and the Allied victory in the Gulf War created international conditions conducive to reaching an Arab–Israeli peace on this basis— and it was from this consensual position that Israel opened negotiations with all its neighbors at the Madrid Peace Conference in 1991.

But the rise of the Labor government in Israel in June 1992 produced a drastic change in Israeli foreign policy. Naïvely dismissing the PLO's professed ultimate aims as "propaganda for internal consumption," the Labor government attempted for the first time to grant many of the PLO's demands—in the hope of being able to forge an alliance with it. At Oslo, Israel in effect accepted the first stage of the PLO's Phased Plan: a gradual withdrawal to the pre-1967 border and the creation of the conditions for an independent PLO state on its borders (except for Jerusalem and the other Jewish communities in Judea and Samaria, which were left for later negotiation).

The first step in the Israeli withdrawal was the evacuation of the Israeli administration and military presence from Gaza. The Gaza district is a narrow strip of land along the Mediterranean some forty miles southwest of Tel Aviv, with a population of about 800,000 Palestinian Arabs, half of them refugees, and with a history of terrorism which competes with that of Lebanon. Egypt occupied Gaza during the Israeli War of Independence in 1948, and controlled the district for nineteen years. During this period, the Palestinian Arabs of Gaza were denied Egyptian citizenship—as compared with Palestinian Arabs living in lands captured by Israel and Jordan in 1948, who were immediately granted citizenship by those two countries. But this did not mean that Gaza was not useful to Nasserist Egypt. In the 1950s, Gaza became the foremost base for *fedayeen*, terrorists backed by the Egyptian government, who staged murderous cross-border raids into Israel resulting in hundreds of deaths and casualties. When Gaza fell into Israel's hands during the 1967 Six-Day War, the city was in a state of appalling underdevelopment, and continued to be one of the principal centers of terrorist activity until 1970, when a concerted action by Israel uprooted most of the active terrorist cells from the area. While Gaza's economy grew over 400 percent in the subsequent years of Israeli administration,[2] the most ambitious Israeli efforts to dismantle the refugee camps and move the residents into modern and permanent housing projects met with ferocious resistance from the PLO, which relied on the system of refugee camps to foster anti-Israel hatred and provide the organization with a steady stream of recruits for its terrorist activities. In the end, only about 11,000 families were moved into the new apartment blocks.

Over the years, Gaza has become a symbol to Israelis as a lair of some of the most rabid Jew-haters in the Middle East. Despite a rich Jewish history, Gaza has become a byword for a hostile and alien place, one of the few bits of land taken by Israel in the Six-Day War of which many Israelis would be pleased to rid themselves. For this reason it was chosen by the Oslo negotiators as the most likely spot to be transferred to the hands of Yasir Arafat as an "empirical" experiment to prove that a PLO state on Israel's borders would be a step toward peace. Gaza was thus handed over to the PLO along with the village of Jericho (population 15,000), as the first step in implementing the Oslo accords between Israel and the PLO. It was there that, in 1994, Yasir Arafat and tens of thousands of his followers arrived, triumphantly waving assault rifles and PLO flags, declaring Arafat to be

"President of Palestine," calling for continued *jihad* until the liberation of Jerusalem, and imposing their corrupt and despotic order on the Arab residents of the area.

Oslo was, of course, celebrated with unrelieved pomp the world over as a great boon to peace, a breakthrough equal to the Egyptian–Israeli peace treaty. Israeli Prime Minister Yitzhak Rabin, Foreign Minister Shimon Peres, and PLO Chairman Yasir Arafat were awarded the Nobel Peace Prize in Oslo, the same city in which negotiations for the PLO–Israel deal were secretly negotiated a year earlier. Under these accords, Israel was to withdraw in stages from all the populated areas in the West Bank and Gaza, and the PLO would set up a regime ostensibly called "autonomy," but which in effect would have nearly all the trappings and attributes of a sovereign state: its own army (called a "police force"); its own executive, legislative, and judicial branches (all of them controlled by Arafat); its own flag, passports, stamps, and border authorities. The PLO in turn promised to annul the PLO Covenant, which calls for Israel's destruction, and to act resolutely to quell any terrorist attacks emanating from PLO-controlled areas.

Shortly after Israel withdrew from Gaza, it became abundantly clear that the PLO had no intention of fulfilling any of its commitments under the Oslo agreement. Arafat refused to convene the Palestine National Council to annul the PLO Covenant, daily generating new excuses until the Israeli government even stopped asking. Equally, it became apparent that far from taking action against terrorist organizations in Gaza, the PLO presided over a fantastic explosion of anti-Israel terrorism from Gaza that threatened to turn its mini-state there into a replica of the PLO mini-state in the Lebanon of the 1970s. Within a year and a half after Oslo, the agreement heralded by the Labor government as "the end to terror," acts of terror against Israel had reached unprecedented dimensions. In the first eighteen months after Oslo, 123 Israelis were killed in terrorist attacks, many of them launched from Gaza, as compared to sixty-seven in the comparable period before Oslo.[3] This was more than double the casualties in terrorist attacks during any comparable period in the preceding two decades—proportionately as if 6,000 Americans had died from terror attacks in a year and a half.

To understand the true intentions of Yasir Arafat and the rest of the PLO leadership, one had only to listen to what they were saying in Arabic to their own people. Several days before the signing of the Oslo accords in Washington, Arafat gave an interview in which he interpreted the event for his followers, telling them that the Oslo accord was the implementation of the Phased Plan decided upon in 1974: "[The agreement] will be a basis for an independent Palestinian state in accordance with the Palestine National Council [of the PLO] resolution issued in 1974."[4] This was the same position elaborated by Abbas Zaki, one of the PLO's security chiefs in the newly "liberated" territories: "This is merely a cease-fire before the next stage . . . I am for negotiations, but they are not the only means. The revolutionaries in Algeria and Vietnam talked peace and fought at the same time"[5]—that is, just as the FLN "talked peace" before completely driving the French out of Algeria, and just as the North Vietnamese "talked peace" before completely driving the United States out of Vietnam (peace talks for which Henry Kissinger and his Vietnamese counterpart were granted the Nobel Peace Prize), so, too, could the PLO talk peace until Israel had been completely driven out of "Palestine"—which is to say, all of Israel. The overly blunt Zaki was discounted as having fallen from grace with Arafat. But to no avail. Arafat's confidants kept making the same points. When Jericho was evacuated by Israel, the commander of the PLO forces entering the city announced: "In Jericho we have taken the first step in the direction of Jerusalem, which will be returned to us in spite of the intransigence of the Zionists."[6] PLO Foreign Minister Farouq Kaddoumi granted an interview in which he added: "The Palestinian people know that there is a state [Israel] that was founded by compulsion of history, and that this state must be brought to an end."[7] Arafat later dropped the metaphor and told the leadership of his "Force 17" Fatah group in Gaza (which includes a highly regarded terrorist leader known by the name "Abu Hitler"): "With blood, fire, and sweat will we liberate Palestine and its capital, Jerusalem."[8] A few days later he added: "In 1974 we accepted the decision [the Phased Plan] to establish our rule over every territory that will be freed from Israeli rule, and we will fulfill this decision."[9] The day before he had said: "We will establish Palestinian authority over every place that will be liberated from the

Zionist enemy. We have achieved the first stage, but the way remains long and hard. We will continue our march until we can fly our flag over Jerusalem, the capital of our country, Palestine."[10] One of the leaders of Arafat's security services in Jericho, Abu al-Fahd, put it more simply: "We will continue the struggle for the liberation of Jerusalem, Haifa, and Beit Shean"[11]—in other words, all of Israel.

With this kind of policy, it is no wonder that soon after Israel's withdrawal the various terrorist groups headquartered in Gaza understood that the time had come for an unprecedented murder spree against Israel. Downtown Jerusalem and central Tel Aviv became the scenes of horrible carnage as buses exploded and crowds of pedestrians were mowed down by machine-gun fire. The same happened in the Israeli towns of Hadera, Afula, and Ashdod, and at Beit Lid near Netanya. Virtually no part of the country was safe. Some of these murders were carried out by PLO operatives, whom Arafat did not discipline in any way. Most were conducted by two Islamic movements in Gaza, Hamas and the Islamic Jihad, which dramatically expanded their operations after the Israeli withdrawal. Here, finally, they had nothing to fear. They could hatch their plans, arm their killers, dispatch them to Israel, and receive those that came back with no fear whatsoever of Israeli reprisal or interception. For as part of the Oslo accords, the Israeli government agreed, incredibly, to give up on the right of "hot pursuit" and preemptive attacks against terrorists, principles that had guided all previous Israeli governments and which Israel continues to apply against the bases of the militant Islamic organization Hizballah in Lebanon. Instead, Israel now relied on Arafat's promise to act against terrorism—thereby creating the only place in the world in which Islamic terrorists would enjoy the promise of immunity from Israeli retaliation.

Not coincidentally, this immunity facilitated an expansion of an Islamic fundamentalist specialty—the suicide attack. That these fundamentalists inculcate young men (mostly disturbed social misfits) to immolate themselves and their victims for the greater glory of Allah is well known. What is less well known is that the more deadly of these attacks, those that require fairly sophisticated explosives and planning, are seldom carried out by solitary individuals. A whole array of people inculcate the suicide, provide him with explosives, guide him in their use, select the chosen target, arrange for his undetected arrival there, and promise to take care of his family after the deed is done. In short, suicide attacks require a significant infrastructure, and the people who provide it are anything but suicidal. On the contrary, they very much want to live; they want to kill, and not be killed. And it is these suicide factories that sprang up in Gaza, free of any fear of retribution from Israel, and which, alongside the more conventional forms of murder by more conventionally minded terrorists, claimed an increasing price in Israeli lives.

But what of Arafat's promise to uproot these terrorists from their strongholds? For nearly two years following the Oslo accords he did not apprehend a single perpetrator of terrorist acts, even though some of the known murderers were serving in his own "police." Though the Israeli security forces provided him lists of known perpetrators, and though his police force had ballooned into an army of 16,000 armed men—per capita ten times the police force of Israel—Arafat did practically nothing to rein in terror. Following Arafat's arrival in Gaza, the Israeli government made more than a dozen requests for extradition of known murderers, many of them serving in the PLO "police"—including Sammy Abu Samadana, murderer of more than thirty Palestinian Arabs and at least one Israeli, now a commander in the PLO police; and the brothers Abu Sita, who murdered an Israeli in March 1993 and are now active in the police force. Indeed, the entire "Fatah Hawks" terrorist organization was incorporated into the PLO police en masse, despite the fact that its members continued terrorist attacks against Israeli citizens well *after* the signing of the Oslo accords.[12] Arafat's refusal to extradite to Israel fourteen Palestinians wanted for murder prompted the legal advisor of the Labor government to state that "this refusal by the Palestinian Authority is a violation of the Oslo accords."[13] Further, the people Arafat appointed to fight the Palestinian terrorists included some of the most savage killers on the PLO's roster of terrorists, including Amin al Hindi, one of the masterminds of the Munich Massacre who now became head of the PLO's "general intelligence service."[14]

The awarding of the Nobel Peace Prize to Yasir Arafat—who more than anyone else alive contributed to the spread of international terrorism, who presides over an organization whose central and guiding political idea remains the desruction of Israel, and who personally presided over countless atrocities against civilians of virtually every nationality in the free world in the service of this goal—is without question the lowest point in the history of the prize, and one which vitiates it of any moral worth. The utter moral obtuseness of the decision to grant Arafat this honor caused the resignation from the Nobel committee of one of its five members, Norwegian Member of Parliament Kaare Kristiansen—the first person on the Nobel committee ever to leave it in protest over an impending award. (Fifty-five years earlier, it had been another Scandinavian, the Swedish senator Brandt, who had half-jokingly recommended awarding the Nobel Peace Prize to Hitler and Chamberlain for the capitulatory "peace" agreement signed at Munich in 1938.[15] But before the Nobel committee could even consider the idea, Hitler upset the applecart by invading what remained of Czechoslovakia. What had been offered in jest in 1939 became a black comedy in 1994.)

If one needs a textbook case on how *not* to fight terrorism, Gaza is it. For if hitherto Israel had shown the world how terrorism could be fought, now it showed how terrorism could be facilitated. From 1993 on, the Israeli government committed many of the mistakes that a state could commit in the war against terror. Its most fundamental mistake, of course, was to capitulate to the terrorists' *political* demands. Seeking relief from PLO terrorism by giving the PLO land, it directly encouraged and emboldened a renewed rash of Islamic terrorism under the PLO umbrella aimed at obtaining even more land. (Later it would negotiate the trading of additional tracts of strategic land for a temporary halt in terror, thereby practically ensuring this terror will reappear once the Palestine state is established and Israeli concessions are stopped.) In Oslo, Israel demonstrated to the PLO and its imitators that terrorism does indeed pay.

Equally, the Israeli government severely impaired its *operational capacity* to fight terrorism by committing no fewer than six classic blunders:

1. It tried to *subcontract the job of fighting terrorism* to someone else—in this case to the terrorists themselves.
2. It *tied the hands of its security forces* by denying them the right to enter or strike at terrorist havens, thus creating inviolable domains for terrorist actions.
3. It *released thousands of jailed terrorists into these domains*, many of whom promptly took up their weapons and returned to ply their trade.
4. It *armed the terrorists*, by enabling the unrestricted flow of thousands of weapons into Gaza, which soon found their way into the hands of the myriad militias and terrorist gangs.
5. It *promised safe passage* for terrorists by exempting PLO VIPs from inspection at the border crossings from Egypt and Jordan, thus enabling the smuggling

of terrorists into Gaza and Jericho, and from there into Israel itself.[16]

6. It *betrayed its Palestinian Arab informants,* many of whom were murdered by the PLO, leaving Israel without an invaluable source of intelligence against terrorist operations in the evacuated areas.

All these errors produced one essential outcome: Gaza became a zone in which terrorism could operate without fear of retribution. Just as free-trade zones encourage trade, the creation of any "free-terror zone" is bound to encourage terrorism. To understand how Gaza under the PLO facilitated terror, it is enough to imagine how terrorism would multiply in the United States if, say, Wichita, Kansas, were a free-terror zone, Gaza-style. After the bombing in Oklahoma City, Timothy McVeigh, or others like him, could escape to this inviolable domain. The FBI could not enter it. The local police would shield, rather than apprehend, the terrorists. Extradition would be out of the question. It is not hard to see that under such conditions all the sundry terrorists and demented loonies in North America would flock to Wichita, quickly transforming it into the terrorist capital of the continent, and another head of the hydra of international terrorism as well. The creation of even semi-free enclaves for terrorists—where the authorities struggle against a substantial pro-terrorist sympathy in the population—such as in Northern Ireland or in the Basque region of Spain, creates horrendous conditions for the security services trying to uproot terrorism. This is why, although the campaigns against terrorist groups in France, Italy, and Germany were ultimately highly successful, Britain and Spain could never quite succeed in eradicating the scourge.

After increasingly bloody and savage attacks emanating from Gaza began to turn Israeli public opinion against further Israeli withdrawals, and after Israel's closure of its cities to Gazan workers imposed economic hardship on his regime, Arafat had to show Israel that he was doing *something* against terrorism. Brushing aside demands that he take forceful action against terrorists from Gaza, he staged instead mock detentions of a cadre of regular Islamic detainees, releasing most of them within days, all the while offering feeble circumlocutions to pass as condemnations of terror. Arafat reneged, too, on his promise to disarm the Islamic movements—in Gaza alone, Hamas and the Palestinian Islamic Jihad have thousands of men under arms. After some internal scuffling between the PLO and these groups threatened to explode into full-scale conflict, Arafat quickly shifted gears and proceeded instead to seek a strategic alliance with the militants, pleading with them that a tactical pause in their terrorist activities would enable the Rabin government to hand over more territory to the PLO, from which the Islamic groups could resume even more intense attacks at a later date.[17] Thus a clear pattern was established. As long as Israel continued to hand over additional land, the relative diminution in terrorism would continue. As soon as Israel stopped its withdrawals, the terror campaign would be resumed in full force.

A momentary suspension of terrorist attacks is not to be confounded with actual dismantling of terrorist capacities, and many Israelis, familiar as they are with the endless stratagems of the terrorist organizations, do not confuse the two. Yet it is difficult for many outside Israel to accept the failings built into the Oslo accords, especially since so many hopes for peace have been vested in these agreements. At the time of the signing of the accords, my party and I were virtually isolated in our warnings that Arafat would not keep his word and that his was merely a tactical peace and not a genuine one. We were widely castigated as enemies of peace, somewhere between the Hizballah and Hamas on the inane scale of categorizations that typify discussions about Israel in the Western media. Oslo was peace. If you were for it, you were for peace. If you were against it, you were against peace. Of course, our argument was that handing Gaza over to Arafat would immediately create a lush terrorist haven and safe house a few miles from Tel Aviv. As I had written a few months before Oslo: "Gaza's security significance rests on its proximity to Israel's cities and on its dense urban center, both of which make it a natural lair for terrorists staging attacks against civilians. In fact, Gaza consistently served this purpose during the nineteen years it was under Egyptian rule."[18]

When the Oslo deal was signed, my party and I repeated this warning, but much of the public at first dismissed our arguments. Only a year and a half later did the situation become so intolerable that even Israel's president, Ezer Weizman, and leading commentators of the

Israeli left were ready to declare that at the very least Israel should suspend the next phase of the Oslo accords and rethink the wisdom of handing over parts of the West Bank, ten minutes away from the outskirts of Tel Aviv, to a PLO army and to the Islamic terrorists. A few ministers in the Labor government echoed these doubts, thereby contributing to a growing mood of public skepticism which threatened the continued implementation of the Oslo accords. The PLO's scheme for achieving a Palestinian state on the strategic mountains overlooking a truncated Israel appeared in jeopardy. Arafat reintensified his pleading with the Islamic militants, offering Hamas a share in future political powers while explaining that the common long-term goal of vanquishing Israel would now best be served by a hiatus in terrorist activities. Finally, after months of intense negotiations between Hamas and the PLO, an understanding was arrived at between the leadership of both movements. The Hamas militants agreed to ease up on terrorism, or at least not to wage it in and around Gaza, so as to permit Arafat to extend the Palestinian domains to the suburbs of Israel's major cities. As they made clear to Arafat, in no way did they give up their plan to fully resume the "armed struggle" once the additional territories had been procured. A senior Israeli military officer described this suspension of violence as a "temporary respite" aimed at "consolidating political gains." Further, the PLO–Hamas understanding did not prevent lower echelons of militants from continued terrorist attacks, some of which (like the July 1995 suicide bombing of an Israeli bus in downtown Ramat Gan) continued to exact a growing toll of innocent Israeli lives. The Israeli Army's Deputy Chief of Intelligence explained that "he feared that once the Israeli Army evacuated West Bank towns, they too might become terrorist havens";[19] moreover, even if Arafat actually took real steps to prevent the launching of terrorist attacks against Israel from the cities handed over to him, "the Palestinian Authority [PLO] would lose any motivation to fight terrorism once Israel withdrew from those cities."[20] Yet it was this tactical interlude between bouts of terror which has been celebrated by enthusiasts the world over as proof of the success of Oslo, and of Arafat's success in "pacifying" Gaza.

If the tactical halt in terrorist attacks agreed upon by Hamas and the PLO holds, it will spell an important development in the relations between the two organizations. As one of the PLO leaders explained, both the PLO and Hamas share the basic strategic goal of doing away with Israel, but they differed on the method of achieving that goal: "[Hamas says] all of Palestine is ours, and we want to liberate it from the river to the sea in one blow. But [Yasir Arafat's] Fatah, which leads the PLO, feels that the Phased Plan must be pursued. Both sides agree on the final objective. The difference between them is on the way to get there."[21] As we have seen, the PLO has been working to eliminate that difference in tactics as well, arguing with Hamas to adopt the PLO's phased approach to eliminating Israel. Needless to say, the PLO did not formally annul its Phased Plan, and no such revocation was even requested by Israel at Oslo.

And as Arafat made clear several times on PLO television, the peace with Israel was little more than the temporary peace agreement that the prophet Muhammad made with the Koreish tribe (Muhammad proceeded to tear that treaty to shreds when he amassed enough strength to annihilate the entire tribe root and branch).[22] What this means is that the negotiations which Israel is now conducting with the PLO over the future of additional territories abutting Tel Aviv and in Jerusalem itself are *de facto* being conducted over land that will be used one day to attack the Jewish state. And Israel's negotiating partners are the allies and protectors of the most militant and radical elements in the Middle East—that is, a PLO which enthusiastically supported Saddam during the Gulf War and which today shields the most ardent champions of militant Islam. Gaza has already been transformed into one of the leading centers of pro-Teheran sentiment outside Iran, and Israel's Labor government is now negotiating over the creation of other such domains, justifying this policy with the contrived suspension of Hamas terrorism. Speaking in January 1995 before Palestinian workers in Gaza, Arafat glorified the suicide bombers: "We are all ready to be *Shaheedeen* [suicide martyrs] on the road to liberate Jerusalem." On June 19, 1995, Arafat emphasized that his basic goal remained unchanged after Oslo: "Our commitment stands and our oath remains. We will continue the hard and long *jihad*, the road of death, the path of sacrifice." As Freh Abu Medien, the PLO's "justice minister," put it on May 8, 1995: "Israel will remain the principal enemy of the Palestinian people, not only today but also in the future."[23]

All this flies in the face of the PLO's solemn pledge under the Oslo agreement "to advance mutual understanding and tolerance . . . and to take legal steps against incitement by individuals and organizations under its jurisdiction" (Item XII [1]). Thus the fostering of public education for coexistence and reconciliation, so indispensable for inducing the psychological changes needed to prevent a future renewal of terrorism and war, are starkly and painfully absent in the PLO domains.

All this has disturbing implications not only for Israel but for the rest of the free world as well. First, a clear linkage was established early on between the Islamic terrorists in Gaza and the cadres of their co-religionists in the United States and Europe, who send money and directives to Gaza on a regular basis. (Such linkages could be reversed, of course, and Hamas could easily send operatives to the West.) A second deadly linkage was unwittingly facilitated by the Israeli government itself, tying the Sunni and Shiite vintages of Islamic radicalism in a tight operational knot. In 1992, before Oslo, the government of Yitzhak Rabin expelled four hundred Hamas Sunni activists from Gaza to south Lebanon. There they were met by their Hizballah Shiite counterparts, who gladly instructed them in the terrorist arts of car bombing, explosives manufacture, and suicide missions. A solid link was thus forged between the two movements, including the detailing of liaison officers. At the time, the Rabin government gave in to the Western outcry against its measures and returned these expelled activists to Gaza after less than a year, in exchange for a farcical written pledge that they would not engage in terrorism. Many of the returnees promptly set up shop in Gaza. Led by Yihya Ayash, otherwise known as "the Engineer," they dispatched terror squads armed with explosives, some of them suicide missions, to attack Israel's cities.

Gaza under Arafat has thus become a unique Islamic base, with solid links in two directions—westward to the United States and Europe, eastward (through Hizballah) to Iran. It can serve in the future as a clearinghouse and stepping-stone for a flexible terrorism launched in multiple directions. Understandably, many Israelis do not want to see that base expanded twenty times to include the West Bank, thereby having an Iranian-influenced Islamic domain hovering over its major cities, and within ten miles of the sea. Such a PLO–Hamas state would sooner or later threaten to topple the pro-Western Hashemite regime in Jordan, the majority of whose population is composed of Palestinian Arabs, many of them susceptible to the fundamentalist message. A Palestinian–Islamic state on the West Bank of the Jordan River might soon expand to include its East Bank as well (i.e., the present state of Jordan), thereby creating a much enlarged base for militant Islam in the heart of the Arab world. Such a base would threaten Syria from the south and Saudi Arabia from the north; through Gaza's geographic contiguity with Egypt on the east, it will have a physical bridge to North Africa, which is already being assaulted by Islamic fundamentalism from the west.

Above all, such a PLO–Hamas state is likely to eventually deteriorate into a new avatar of the PLO terror-state in Lebanon, which was responsible for the exportation of terrorism far beyond the Middle East, serving as a convenient relay station and launching ground for the growing Islamic terrorism against Western targets. This will not necessarily happen overnight. It may take several years for such a state to reveal its true nature. It might first wish to build up its power, adopting a relatively docile outward appearance to continue receiving Western aid and further Israeli concessions. But the underlying irredentist and terrorist impulses that are at the core of its political ideology and *raison d'être* are unfortunately not likely to disappear.

Even now, it is possible to correct the mistakes which the Labor government has made in its efforts to appease Palestinian terror. Stability may be achieved and terrorism put on the defensive if Israel reassumes responsibility for its own security and asserts a policy of local autonomy for the Palestinian Arabs instead of the independent terror-free zones now being built. It will take some time for the rest of the world to understand what many in Israel now know: that far from producing the durable peace all Israelis yearn for, the continued expansion of an armed, independent Palestinian domain is merely a stepping-stone to the eventual escalation of conflict and the continued march of Islamic militancy in the Middle East and beyond.

VI

The Specter of Nuclear Terrorism

Yet there is one other potential development that could overshadow all this. The expansion of militant Islam, its growing power to intimidate the West and to cause it grievous damage, would be immeasurably increased if the Islamic Republic of Iran or the Sunni militant movement succeeded in acquiring nonconventional weapons—chemical, biological, or even nuclear. The best estimates at this time place Iran between three and five years away from possessing the prerequisites required for the independent production of nuclear weapons. After this time, the Iranian Islamic republic will have the ability to construct atomic weapons without the importation of materials or technology from abroad.

Iran has two nuclear reactor sites. The first, at Busheir, was supplied by West Germany when Iran was still ruled by the Shah. Work at the Busheir plant was stopped in 1979 with the seizure of the government by the Ayatollah Khomeini. At this point, construction of the plant was roughly 85 percent complete, and the special electrical work necessary for such installations was approximately 65 percent complete. The reactor at Busheir was bombed by Saddam Hussein during the Iran–Iraq war (which of course did not stop Saddam from condemning the Israeli attack on *his* nuclear reactor at Osiraq). After the end of the Iran–Iraq war in 1992, Iran signed an agreement with post-Soviet Russia for the revitalization of the site. The agreement called for the Russians to supply Iran with two 440-megawatt reactors. In early 1995 it was agreed that two other reactors which had been slated for construction in northern Iran were also to be moved to Busheir. The first phase of construction and electrical work will be completed within three to four years. A second project is under way in northern Iran at Darku-bin. In the days of the Shah, Iran had signed a contract with France to provide two reactors at this site, and this work, too, was halted by the outbreak of the war with Iraq. In 1993, Iran reached an agreement with China to provide this location with two 300-megawatt reactors, a deal which the United States attempted to block without success. In addition, Iran has its own uranium mine and processing plant at Sighand, which will be operational within three to five years. Finally, Iran has two institutes conducting nuclear research; the principal one at Isfahan is developing techniques for uranium enrichment under the guise of a civilian research project. This means that, within a short time, Iran will have the raw materials, the plants, and the technical know-how to produce its own bombs. It would then be a matter of five to seven years at most before Iran is able to assemble such weapons.

There is no way of knowing whether Iran can be deterred from using its nuclear arsenal, as the Soviet Union was for more than four decades, or whether it would actually be willing to one day plunge the world into the abyss. But whether or not the Iranian regime is in fact willing to use such a device, it is critical to recognize the effect that an "Islamic bomb" in the hands of Iran would immediately have on the *conventional* balance of power in the Middle East—for it would be a "new Middle East" indeed. The acquisition of nuclear weapons by the Islamic republic would dramatically realign the political forces of the Middle East toward heightened radicalism. It would be seen as the greatest of anti-Western weapons, even more powerful than the oil weapon at its height, and a providential sign that Allah had not abandoned his faithful. States such as Algeria, which are in any case tottering on the brink of Islamic revolution, would suddenly find themselves facing a dramatically more powerful domestic threat from their Muslim fanatics. And the peace treaties which Israel has signed may be placed under intolerable pressure under the withering radiation of a nuclear-armed militant Islam. One need only recall how King Hussein—whose commitment to peace with Israel has been demonstrated since 1970—found himself having to make common cause with Saddam Hussein in 1991, when Saddam was at the height of his prestige in the days following Iraq's incursion into Kuwait. Power has its own logic, and such a quantum leap in the power of Islamic radicalism would attract to it millions of new adherents around the world, and much new political support—both that produced by adulation and that produced by fear—throughout the Middle East and far beyond it.

How could Iran use such nuclear weapons? It might, of course, threaten the West or any of its neighbors outright, just as Saddam Hussein would undoubtedly have done had his nuclear programs been completed by the time of his invasion of Kuwait. If Saddam had possessed atomic bombs, the Gulf War probably would never have taken place. He could have made it clear that he was prepared to strike at the Allied forces with nuclear weapons; or that he would destroy a neighboring capital like Riyadh; or that he would destroy the oil-loading facilities of the Persian Gulf; or that he would bomb the Straits of Hormuz, wreaking a catastrophe that would have closed down the sea lanes to much of the world's oil— just as he had no compunction about pouring billions of barrels of oil into the Gulf as a warning to the Allies, in the process inventing a new form of ecological terrorism.

A nuclear-armed Iran such as we may have to face in the coming years will have all these options open in a future confrontation with the West, and others as well. It could avoid a direct threat against the United States and the West with its attendant consequences of horrible retribution. It could instead resort to indirect intimidation of nuclear holocaust, dissociating itself from the threat by using any one of a number of shadowy Islamic terrorist groups that it controls. Such a group could emerge anywhere in the sea of militant Islamic puddles that now cover the entire West. The group could issue a veiled ultimatum that unless demands emanating from Iran were met, it would exact a horrible price. Further, Iran might be tempted to actually *use* nuclear weapons against Israel or a neighboring Arab state, and then avoid the consequences of Western reaction by threatening to activate its pre-armed militants in the West. Such groups nullify in large measure the need to have air power or intercontinental missiles as delivery systems for an Islamic nuclear payload. *They* will be the delivery system. In the worst of such scenarios, the consequences could be not a car bomb but a *nuclear* bomb in the basement of the World Trade Center.

This may sound incredible or beyond the realm of possibility. Unfortunately, it is not. Anyone familiar with the warped fanaticism and increasing technical proficiency of Islamic militants cannot rule it out as a growing danger. Today's terrorist groups can already deploy chemical weapons of the most lethal variety known to man. Equipped by a runaway terrorist regime, they could be given other, even more deadly, nonconventional weapons.

One does not have to be an expert in international terrorism to sense that this rising tide of Islamic terrorism is qualitatively different from the terrorism which the West has had to face up until now. For it derives from a highly irrational cultural source, militant Islam, which differs profoundly from that other anti-Western doctrinaire militancy, Communism. Some similarities between the two movements are striking. Both have sought world dominion in the service of an all-encompassing ideology. Both have had millions of adherents spread around the globe ready to do their bidding. Both have been centered in a home country, which organized the dissemination of the creed worldwide. Yet the similarities end there. For while the Communists pursued an irrational doctrine, they nonetheless pursued it rationally. Neither Stalin nor Brezhnev ever seriously considered putting ideology above existence. This is why the Communists eventually accepted the necessity of co-existence. When it came to deciding between blowing themselves up in a nuclear exchange and compromising on their ideology, they could be counted on to compromise on their ideology every time.

The trouble with militant Islam is that it appears to be an irrational goal being pursued *irrationally*. And this irrationality expresses itself in the ease with which the militant Muslims reverse the order of priorities, putting ideological zeal before life itself. The rapidly increasing use of suicide bombings by Islamic terrorists of the Hizballah and Hamas suggests that at least some of the people involved have no qualms about blowing themselves up in the service of their ideology (a phenomenon Americans will remember from the Japanese kamikazes of World War II). This pathology—I can use no other term—manifests itself in the glee with which mothers offer their sons for the greater glory of the faith, or in the ritualistic drinking from fountains of blood by Iranian soldiers during the Iran–Iraq war. Today one must realistically face the possibility that in the not too distant future militant Middle Eastern states will possess nuclear weapons.

That the world is standing in front of an abyss is barely understood by most political leaders today. For the irrational strain that runs through Islamic fundamentalism and its obsessive hatred of the West are usually discounted in assessing its potential threat. But the leaders of the West must take into account that this irrationality might prompt the leaders of Iran to toy with the idea of terrorist blackmail on an unimaginable scale. Once Iran has nuclear weapons, there is nothing to say that it will not move to greater adventurism and irrationality rather than greater responsibility. It is not inconceivable that such a regime, in the throes of an international conflict or internal political convulsion, could threaten the United States, or Britain, or France with nonconventional weapons. If this happens, international terrorism could undergo an incredible transformation in which not individual citizens or buildings are threatened or demolished but entire *cities* are held hostage.

The only way to understand the failure of understanding in this regard is to look back at another hate-filled ideology that began as another local manifestation and within a few years became a global force. Like Islamic fundamentalism, Nazism sixty years ago was directed first against the Jews and other local minorities. But soon it was evident that its creed of hate swept like wildfire throughout all Europe and the world. The Western nations woke up almost too late to its incendiary nature, and to the danger it posed to civilization. But consider what would have happened had Hitler succeeded in his own quest for a nuclear capability. When his scientists invented the V-2 rocket, he had no qualms whatsoever about raining them down in deadly payloads on downtown London. We can only shudder at the consequences for the world if Hitler's mad antipathies had been wedded to nuclear weapons. Our civilization and our culture would have come to an end. Today, for the second time in modern times, we are faced with the possibility that an irrational movement might come into possession of weapons of mass annihilation. This is the greatest terror imaginable, because the greatest danger of nuclear weapons is in the lack of susceptibility of their deployers to sober calculations of cost and benefit. If Iran, or its militant proxies in the Middle East or Europe or the United States, has atomic bombs, we will be faced with a possibility of terrorism and blackmail that would make Oklahoma City look like a children's game. This is the great peril, and it has not been addressed. The democracies have wasted much time. They are approaching the twelfth hour. They can wait no longer.

VII

What Is to Be Done

As by now nearly everyone understands, "history" did not end with the collapse of Soviet Communism. The New World Disorder is not merely a hodgepodge of local nuisances that pose no substantial threat to our civilization and our way of life. True, the disintegration of the Soviet Union removed the ideological impetus of Communist domination, but it also lifted the staying hand that the Kremlin had exercised against the ambitions of many local clients and petty dictators. Further, the disappearance of Communist rule in the Kremlin opened up the spigot of nuclear technology that now flows from the impoverished remnants of the Soviet Union to anyone willing and able to pay for it; and the great spiritual and political void created by the evaporation of Communism has at least partly paved the way for the accelerating march of militant Islam in many parts of the Middle East and elsewhere that had previously toyed with Communism as a creed worthy of embracing.

The second wave of international terrorism, that of the 1990s, is the direct result of all these developments. And the growth of militant Islamic terrorism, with independent states in the Middle East serving as its launching ground and bases of Islamic militants in the West offering alternate bridgeheads, has already been felt in the West in more ways than one. Just as Soviet-Arab terrorism produced its imitators, so, too, the growth of this kind of chaos is bound to have an effect on its would-be imitators. It may not be pure coincidence that the method used to bomb the federal building in Oklahoma City was a mimicry of the favorite type of Islamic fundamentalist car bombing. If this kind of domestic international terrorism is not cut out at the root, it is bound to grow, with disastrous consequences.

Undoubtedly the two greatest obstacles to dealing with this problem are, first, recognizing the nature of the threat and, second, understanding that it can be defeated. My first intention in writing this book has been, accordingly, to alert the citizens and decision-makers of the West as to the nature of the new terrorist challenge which the democracies now face. In this time of historic flux, Western leaders have a responsibility to resist the tendency for passivity, the temptation to rest on the laurels of the victory over Communism as though nothing else truly could jeopardize their societies. The leaders of the democracies must solicit the understanding and support of the public and its elected representatives for vigorous policies against terrorism. *Obsta principiis*—oppose bad things when they are small—was the motto of Israel

Zangwill, one of the first leaders of the modern Jewish national movement at the beginning of this century. Alas, many of his colleagues did not heed this warning, and the Jewish people paid a horrendous price in the decades that followed. The same advice must be directed today to presidents and prime ministers, congressmen and parliamentarians, with one proviso: When it comes to terrorism, the bad things are no longer small. They have already reached disturbing proportions, though it must be said that they have not yet grown to dimensions that prevent them from being contained and defeated with relatively little cost.

Which brings me to my second point. Once the nature of the threat is understood, the Western countries must understand that it can be fought effectively. Rather than adopting an attitude of dismissive or fatalistic acceptance, this book is a plea for action, which, if prosecuted resolutely and consistently, is bound to remove the threat or at least substantially reduce it. Of necessity, such action falls into the two domains we have been discussing: the international and the domestic. And as we have seen, because of the growing linkages between the two, these domains are not mutually exclusive. Action on the international level against terrorism impedes its domestic offshoots, and vice versa.

I begin with actions which must be taken on the international level, because, as I have repeatedly stressed throughout, this is where the main danger comes from. It is the offending terrorist regimes which provide today's international terrorists with the moral and material support without which they would not dare attack Western societies. What follows is a series of measures which could be effectively undertaken by democracies to stamp out terrorism within their own borders. This is what American administrators and lawmakers began to do in a systematic way only with the Omnibus Counter-Terrorism Act of 1995, a Clinton administration initiative forged in the wake of the Oklahoma City bombing. Other leading democracies must follow this lead and reconsider their own positions as well.

1. Impose sanctions on suppliers of nuclear technology to terrorist states. The United States must lead the Western world in preventing the proliferation of nuclear technology, fissionable materials, and nuclear scientists to Iran and any other regime with a history of practicing terrorism. While such action under UN supervision has been taken against Iraq in the wake of the Gulf War, little or no action was taken until recently against the Iranian nuclear program. Israeli efforts to warn of the danger of the Iranian nuclear program and the Clinton administration's moves to prevent Russia from supplying Iran with gas centrifuges should serve as two examples of what needs to be done on a far broader scale. *All* nuclear technology and know-how should be denied to such states, for they will invariably deploy them in the service of their aggressive purposes. It should be noted that all nuclear proliferation is bad, but some of it is worse. Nuclear weapons in the hands of, say, the Dutch government are simply not the same as nuclear weapons in the hands of Qaddafi or the Ayatollahs in Teheran. What I advocate here is of necessity action directed first against the *suppliers* and not the buyers, and it must be led by the United States. The supplying countries must be told bluntly that they must choose between trade with terrorist states and trade with the United States. A special American effort must be made to harness to this regime of anti-nuclear sanctions all the Western countries, as well as Russia, China, Japan, and North Korea. The European countries in particular often hide behind liberal trade laws that enable European companies to engage in such trade without strict government supervision. The United States should insist that those laws be changed; i.e., that free trade, like free speech, has its limits in the supply of laser triggers, gas centrifuges, and enriched uranium.

The United States Congress has successfully pressed for enforcement of other standards of international behavior by denying preferred trade status and other economic favors to states limiting free emigration, sponsoring terrorism, or trafficking in drugs. The Soviet Union was largely moved to permit Soviet Jews to begin emigrating during the 1970s when the Congress passed the Jackson-Vanik Amendment, linking Soviet trade with the United States to freedom of emigration. Similar legislation could create an official list of states supplying nuclear technologies to other countries, which could likewise be subjected to trade sanctions. Countries which have international trading regulations so liberal that they can trade in nuclear death will find themselves having to change their laws or feel the pain where it matters to them most—in their pocketbooks. Such a list should in theory be maintained by the United Nations in order to have maximum effect, but this is not the essence. The main point is that the United States should adopt a firm policy and then proceed to bring other nations on board. And quickly.

2. Impose diplomatic, economic, and military sanctions on the terrorist states themselves. This tested measure has not been applied in any serious fashion to the twin sources of today's militant Islamic terrorism, Iran and Sudan. Where it has been systematically applied, against Libya and Iraq, it has had measurable success. Those regimes have consciously backed off from the energetic sponsorship of terrorism that characterized their conduct in the 1970s and 1980s. In general, the dosage of these sanctions should be on an escalating scale, beginning with closing down embassies, proceeding to trade sanctions, and, if this fails, considering the possibility of military strikes such as those delivered against Libya in 1986, which all but put this fanatical regime out of the terrorism business. While military measures should not be the first option, they should never be excluded from the roster of possibilities. The mere knowledge by a terrorist state that it is opening itself up to the possibility of painful and humiliating military reprisals may be enough to cool the heels of dictators entertaining the thought of undertaking terrorist campaigns against the West or its allies. Iran in particular is susceptible to economic pressure. The oil-exporting Islamic republic is virtually a single-crop economy, and imposition of a tight blockade against Iranian oil sales will undoubtedly induce in Teheran a prompt reevaluation of the utility of even indirect terrorist tactics.

Similarly, the special exemption hitherto granted to Syria must be brought to an end. It is not enough anymore that Syria merely continues to appear on Washington's list of states sponsoring terror. Over a dozen terrorist groups are openly housed in Damascus, and many have training facilities in the Syrian-controlled Bekaa Valley in Lebanon. These groups prosecute terrorist campaigns against Israel, as well as Jewish and non-Jewish targets throughout the world. The U.S. State Department's own 1994 report on terrorism mentions among these groups Ahmed Jibril's Popular Front for the Liberation of Palestine–General Command (PFLP–GC), Hamas, the Palestinian Islamic Jihad, the Japanese Red Army, and the Kurdish PKK.[1] The idea that one of the most unrelenting of terrorist regimes should be exempted from sanctions so as not to "offend" its leader and harm the "prospects of peace" is an absurdity. Both the Soviet Union's Iron Curtain and South Africa's odious system of racial laws were eventually brought down by a firm Western policy of linking sanctions to an improvement in Soviet and South African policies, and there is no reason that a much less powerful state such as Syria should be any less responsive when faced with determined pressure over a protracted period. The tendency to try and bribe Syria to desist from its support for terrorism—with American aid and Israeli concessions on the Golan Heights—is the exact opposite of what is needed. As in the case of the PLO in Gaza, the most that can be hoped for from buying off Syria is a tactical cessation of its proxy terrorism aimed at extracting the latest round of concessions; in this case, the terror inevitably resumes once these concessions have been digested and it looks like the next round is to be had. The cessation of terrorism must therefore be a clear-cut demand, backed up by sanctions and with no prizes attached. As with all international efforts, the vigorous application of sanctions to terrorist states must be led by the United States, whose leaders must choose the correct sequence, timing, and circumstances for these actions.

3. Neutralize terrorist enclaves. Efforts must be made to stop terrorism from areas that are less than independent states but nevertheless serve as breeding grounds for terrorists. The most notable include the Hizballah enclave in southern Lebanon, the PLO–Hamas fiefdom in Gaza, the Kurdish PKK strongholds in northern Iraq, and the *Mujahdeen* enclave on the Pakistani border with Kashmir. What characterizes all these enclaves is the professed claim of the local government that it is unable to prevent the terrorism launched from its domain. Sometimes, as in Lebanon, this is indeed the case; the Lebanese government is virtually powerless to prevent Hizballah terrorism, but Syria and Iran—which respectively control the territory from which Hizballah operates and which give it funds and ideological backing—are perfectly able to do so. Syria and Iran should therefore be pressed to cease not only terrorism which they sponsor directly from within their own borders but also the proxy terrorism which they protect and encourage from beyond their frontiers.

The same applies to Iranian and Syrian agitation in Gaza, with one crucial difference. Here, the local PLO authority is perfectly capable of undertaking a variety of measures that would totally dismantle rather than buy off Gaza-based terrorist organizations, but refuses to do so. The United States and other Western countries should in turn refuse to transfer any funds to the PLO until it lives up to its part of the Oslo agreement, beginning with a relentless and all-encompassing war against terrorism. And if such activity is still not forthcoming, then it must be understood that Israel will have to take action against the sources of terror, precisely as it does in south Lebanon and anywhere else.

4. Freeze financial assets in the West of terrorist regimes and organizations. This measure was used intermittently by the Carter and Reagan administrations during the American embassy hostage crisis and its aftermath. It should be expanded today to include the assets of militant Islamic groups which keep monies in the United States for the purpose of operating there and elsewhere. In addition, the solicitation and transferring of funds for terrorist activity in the United States and abroad should be absolutely prohibited. Throughout the democracies, the funding of terrorist activity should be considered a form of participation in terrorist acts.

5. Share intelligence. One of the central problems in the fight against international terrorism has traditionally been the hesitation of the security services of one nation to share information with foreign services. In this regard, countries have often viewed "their" terrorists as though they were the only terrorists worth fighting, while turning a blind eye to activities hostile to other governments. The trouble with this method is not only that it is of questionable morality; the fact is that it does not work. Terrorists hide behind the mutual suspicions between the Western security services, seeming to be attacking a particular nation when in fact they often view the entire West as a common society and a common enemy. Only through close coordination between law enforcement officials and the intelligence services of all free countries can a serious effort against international terrorism be successful.

It should be made clear that I am not speaking here of warnings of impending terrorist attacks. Those are now shared instantaneously by virtually all the intelligence agencies of the West. What is not shared is basic data about terrorist organizations, their membership and their operational structure. These "cards" are often withheld from the intelligence services of other countries (and sometimes even from a rival service in the *same* country) for two reasons: either to protect the source of the information or else, at least as often, out of a habitual organizational jealousy. But the absence of systematic sharing of intelligence is not a matter of petty one-upmanship. It greatly hinders each democracy as it struggles alone to get a full picture of terrorist activity directed against its citizens, with the inevitable result that lives are needlessly lost. If the democracies wish to successfully confront the new terrorism, there is no choice but for the scope of intelligence cooperation to be increased, and the scope of the jealousies reduced.

6. Revise legislation to enable greater surveillance and action against organizations inciting to violence, subject to periodic renewal. In countries repeatedly assaulted by terrorism, a thorough review of the legal measures governing the battle against terrorism may become a necessity from time to time. There are those who say, for example, that the existing powers of the security services of the United States are sufficient to enable them to track terrorist threats; others disagree. I do not presume to enter into this legal debate over the specifics of standing American law. Rather, I propose that the laws of every free society must be such as to permit the security services to move against groups which incite to violence against the country's government or its citizens. The test is simple. If the law does not allow a government to sift through the extremist splinters advocating violence in order to identify which groups are actively *planning* terrorist actions and to shut them down *before* they strike, then the law is insufficient.

Legislation should be reviewed and if necessary

revised to facilitate the following measures in all or part, depending on the degree of the terrorist threat facing each society and its particular culture and legal traditions.

- *Outlaw fund-raising and channeling of funds to terrorist groups.* The funding of terrorist activity, both inside and outside a given country, must be made illegal. At present, terrorist groups often "skim" an allocation off charitable funds raised by sympathetic ethnic or religious organizations. Involvement in any stage of this process is tantamount to directly facilitating lethal terror and should be regarded as a crime of that magnitude. The American counter-terror bill more or less takes this step by outlawing fund-raising for any organization designated by the President to be a terrorist group. It does, however, include the bizarre proviso that such terrorist groups may apply for a U.S. government license to fund-raise for those of their activities which are "legitimate." Whether such an approach can have the intended effect of stopping fund-raising for terrorism in America remains to be seen.
- *Permit investigation of groups preaching terror and planning the violent overthrow of the government.* Surveillance of and intelligence gathering on groups exhorting violence and suspected of planning violent attacks must be permitted. If the security services cannot research which groups may be dangerous before they strike, there is little hope of being able to

prevent terrorism from springing up again and again.

• *Loosen warrant requirements in terrorist cases.* Search and seizure, detention, and interrogation may be necessary for short periods without a warrant where there is a strong suspicion of terrorist activity. Strict and prompt judicial oversight of such actions can serve as a sufficient deterrent to most government abuses, but it is important to experiment as many democracies have done with the particular regulations. Law enforcement officials should be given considerable freedom to respond quickly to information as it is brought to light, but they should know that they will be subject to review of their activities after the fact.

• *Restrict ownership of weapons.* Tighten gun control, beginning with registry of weapons. Israeli law, for example, requires careful licensing of handguns and prohibits the ownership of more powerful weapons, yet gun ownership is widespread. Forbidding the ownership of machine guns is not a denial of the right to own a weapon for self-defense; it is a denial of the right to organize private armies—a right which no society can grant without eventually having to fight those armies. The continued existence in the United States of heavily armed anti-government militias numbering thousands of members is a grotesque distortion of the idea of civil freedom, which should be brought to a speedy end.

- *Tighten immigration laws.* It is now well known that terrorists from the Middle East and elsewhere have made the United States, Germany, Italy, and other countries into terrorist havens because of laxity in immigration regulation. This era of immigration free-for-all should be brought to an end. An important aspect of taking control of the immigration situation is stricter background checks of potential immigrants, coupled with the real possibility of deportation. The possibility of expulsion must be a threat hovering over all terrorist and pro-terrorist activity in the democracies. The new Clinton administration initiative, for example, defines spokesmen and fund-raisers for terrorist organizations as liable to deportation, makes immigration files available to federal investigators, and establishes a special judicial process for deportations in which classified evidence may be brought without giving the terrorist organizations access to the materials.

- *Require periodic legislative review to safeguard civil liberties.* The concern of civil libertarians over possible infringements of the rights of innocent citizens is well placed, and all additional powers granted the security services should require annual renewal by the legislature, this in addition to judicial oversight of actions as they are taken in the field. Thus, hearings may be held to consider the record of possible abuses which have resulted from changes in police authority. If the abuses prove to be too frequent or the results inconclusive in terms of the citizens, the particular provisions in question can be jettisoned automatically.

The legal provisions suggested above constitute a roster of measures available to a democracy subjected to a sustained threat of terror. A lesser threat usually could require fewer measures. In some countries, these measures would necessarily mean shifting the legal balance between civil liberties and security. There is nothing easy in making this choice. But it is nevertheless crucial that the citizens of the West understand that such options are legitimately available to them, and that, judiciously applied, they may serve to put terrorism back on the defensive.

7. Actively pursue terrorists. Legal powers are of course meaningless if they are not accompanied by a commensurate mustering of will to act on the part of the executive branch and the security services. Rooting out terrorist groups must become a top priority for elected officials of all parties—and one that cannot be allowed to slide from political relevance after a few cases have been cracked. In an age in which the power of the weapons which individuals may obtain grows incredibly from one year to the next, and in which information about how to obtain and use such weapons can be instantly transmitted by electronic mail from any part of the world, an active internal-security policy and aggressive counter-terrorism actions are becoming a crucial part of the mandate of every government, and officials must learn to rise to this challenge. Potential sources of terror must be studied and understood, groups preaching violence must be penetrated and catalogued, and groups actually preparing for it must be uprooted.

8. Do not release jailed terrorists. Among the most important policies which must be adopted in the face of terrorism is the refusal to release convicted terrorists from prisons. This is a mistake that Israel, once the leader in anti-terror techniques, has made over and over again. Release of convicted terrorists before they have served their full sentences seems like an easy and tempting way of defusing blackmail situations in which innocent people may lose their lives. But its utility is momentary at best. Prisoner releases only embolden terrorists by giving them the feeling that even if they are caught their punishment will be brief. Worse, by leading terrorists to think such demands are likely to be met, they encourage precisely the kind of terrorist blackmail which they are supposed to defuse: All that Timothy McVeigh's compatriots need to know is that the United States government is susceptible to releasing him in exchange for the lives of innocent hostages in order to get the terrorists to make just such a demand; only the most unrelenting refusal to ever give in to such blackmail can prevent most such situations from arising.

9. Train special forces to fight terrorism. Greater emphasis must be placed on the training of special units equipped for anti-terror operations. In anti-terror training, law enforcers learn to fight a completely different kind of gun battle, in which the goal is to *hold* their fire rather than to unleash it. Operations against terrorists often involve the rescue of hostages or the possibility that innocent bystanders might be hurt. This necessarily means that the soldiers or policemen charged with fighting terrorism must learn to subdue the natural temptation to concentrate overwhelming fire on the enemy. Counter-terrorist operations usually require the barest minimum application of force necessary to overcome the terrorists, who often use hostages as a human shield.

While those branches of Western security services specializing in counter-intelligence and surveillance generally enjoy a high level of professionalism and training, this is often not the case with the forces that have to do the actual fighting against terrorists. It may be impossible to guarantee that there will be no more scenes such as the one in Waco, Texas, in which scores of cultists and four lawmen were killed. But the likelihood of avoiding such catastrophes is considerably increased if the forces involved are proficient in anti-terror techniques. Such units at the national or federal level are usually adequately trained for these missions, but in a crisis it may take them many hours to arrive on the scene. It is therefore important that units of local police forces be trained in anti-terror tactics as well.

Israel has had some spectacular successes in this area, including the rescue of 103 hostages at Entebbe. But it has also had its share of spectacular failures, the worst of which was the loss of twenty-six schoolchildren being held hostage in a school building in Maalot. Having specially trained troops that accumulate and refine anti-terror techniques reduces the probability of failure; it does not, of course, mean that terrorists may be fought and hostages rescued without risk. What is crucial to recognize is that the risk to society of *not* challenging the terrorists forcefully—that is, of negotiating with them and accepting their demands—is far greater than the risk involved in the use of special forces. For in negotiating, the government issues an open invitation for more terror, an invitation which puts at risk the safety of every citizen in society.

10. Educate the public. The terrorist uses violence to erode the resistance of the public and leaders alike to his political demands. But the resistance of a society to terrorist blackmail may likewise be *strengthened* by counter-terrorist education, which clearly puts forth what the terrorists are trying to achieve, elucidates the immorality of their methods, and explains the necessity of resisting them. Such education is usually unnecessary in the case of sporadic and isolated terrorist attacks, which are almost universally met with an appropriate and natural revulsion. But in the case of a prolonged and sustained campaign lasting months or years, the natural disgust of the public with the terrorist's message begins to break down and is often replaced by a willingness to accommodate terrorist demands. By preparing terrorism-education programs for various age groups and including them in the school curriculum, the government can inoculate the population against the impulse to give in when faced with protracted terrorist pressure. Familiarity with terrorism and its complete rejection would create a citizenry which is capable of "living with terror"—not in the sense of accepting terror, but rather in the sense of understanding what is needed for society to survive its attacks with the least damage. And once the terrorists know that virtually the entire population will stand behind the government's decision never to negotiate with them, the possibility of actually extracting political concessions will begin to look exceedingly remote to them.[2]

With such a program of steadfast resistance to the rising tide of terror, the United States may once again lead the West, as it did in the 1980s, in successfully fighting terrorism. Of course, much of this program is laced with obstacles that only purposeful determination may overcome. The leaders of Western countries may choose instead to avoid taking the tough decisions and continue doing business as usual; they may adopt few or none of these measures, believing that the new wave of terrorism will somehow dissipate of its own accord. It will not. Terrorism has the unfortunate quality of expanding to fill the vacuum left to it by passivity or weakness. And it shrinks accordingly when confronted with resolute and decisive action. Terrorists may test this resolution a number of times before they draw back, and a government has to be prepared to sustain its anti-terror policies through shrill criticism, anxious calls to give in to terrorists' demands, and even responses of panic. But it is a certainty that there is no way to fight terrorism—other than to fight it.

Undoubtedly the leaders of the United States in particular could be subjected to a barrage of criticism that they are curtailing civil freedoms and that they are overreacting. They should reject this criticism, responding, as has the Supreme Court of the United States, that "it is 'obvious and unarguable' that no governmental interest is more compelling than the security of the Nation"[3]—and this includes unlimited civil liberties. Western democracy is strong enough to be able to monitor any added powers given its security services, especially if the technique of requiring periodic renewal of these powers is adopted. Moreover, the security of the democracies and their well-being cannot be governed by the ebb and flow of local political skirmishes. Leaders must have the courage to do what is required even in the face of the most stinging criticism. Courageous action is in itself the best answer to the inevitable slings that the small-minded heap upon the statesman facing great odds. And seldom has there been a menace that so called for the courage and resolve of the true statesman as the resurgent terror which threatens to rob us of the freedoms and values we so cherish.

NOTES

CHAPTER I

1. Broadcast of March 5, 1995.
2. See *The Economist*, May 5, 1995; *Time*, May 8, 1995; *U.S. News & World Report*, May 8, 1995; *Newsweek*, May 8, 1995.
3. See Benjamin Netanyahu, ed., *Terrorism: How the West Can Win* (New York: Farrar, Straus and Giroux, 1986).

CHAPTER II

1. Christian Lochte, "Fighting Terrorism in the Federal Republic of Germany" in *Terrorism: How the West Can Win*, p. 173.
2. Joseph W. Bishop, "Legal Measures to Control Terrorism in Democracies," in Benjamin Netanyahu, ed., *International Terrorism: Challenge and Response* (New Brunswick, NJ: Transaction, 1981), p. 301.
3. Yigal Carmon, former Prime Minister's adviser on terrorism.
4. Bishop, pp. 302–4.
5. Quoted in Walter Berns, "Constitutional Power and the Defense of Free Government," in *Terrorism: How the West Can Win*.
6. Ibid.
7. Benedict de Spinoza, *A Theological-Political Treatise*, R.H.M. Elwes, trans. (New York: Dover, 1951), pp. 258, 260.

Notes

CHAPTER III

1. Richard Pipes, "The Roots of the Involvement," in *International Terrorism: Challenge and Response,* pp. 58–61.
2. Michael Ledeen, "Soviet Sponsorship: The Will to Disbelieve," in *Terrorism: How the West Can Win*, pp. 88–92.
3. Brian Crozier, "Soviet Support for International Terrorism," in *International Terrorism: Challenge and Response*, pp. 66–68.
4. Ray Cline, "The Strategic Framework," in *International Terrorism: Challenge and Response*, p. 94.
5. Ledeen, p. 91.
6. Ibid., p. 90. See also Benjamin Netanyahu, *A Place Among the Nations: Israel and the World* (New York: Bantam, 1993), pp. 194–95. Documentation for the PLO's relationship with the Soviet Union, as well as with other terrorist groups serving as proxy warriors in a host of countries, can be found in Uri Ra'anan, *et al.*, *Hydra of Carnage: International Links of Terrorism* (Lexington, MA: Heath, 1986), pp. 477–568, 609–20.
7. Crozier, p. 70.
8. *The Wall Street Journal*, July 26, 1979.
9. Benjamin Netanyahu, "Defining Terrorism," in *Terrorism: How the West Can Win*, pp. 16–17, 23.
10. George P. Shultz, *Turmoil and Triumph: My Years as Secretary of State* (New York: Charles Scribner's Sons, 1993), p. 790.

CHAPTER IV

1. Muhammad Nuwayhi, *Towards a Revolution in Religious Thought* (1907), excerpted in John Donohue and John Esposito, eds., *Islam in Transition: Muslim Perspectives* (New York: Oxford, 1982), pp. 167–68.
2. Netanyahu, *A Place Among the Nations: Israel and the World*, p. 122.
3. Arafat quoted in Saudi News Agency, January 2, 1989.
4. This discussion of the Muslim Arab view of history adapted from Netanyahu, *A Place Among the Nations*, pp. 107–23.

Notes

5. *Yediot Aharonot*, June 27, 1995.
6. Source for militant Islamic activity in Europe, except where otherwise indicated: Yigal Carmon, formerly Adviser to the Prime Minister on Terror.
7. *Jihad in America*, pp. 13, 21, 7.

CHAPTER V

1. The Phased Plan was adopted by the Palestine National Council (PNC), the parent body of the PLO, on June 8, 1974. It declares that "the PLO is fighting by every means . . . to free the Palestinian land and establish a national, independent, and fighting government over every part of the soil of Palestine to be freed" [Section 2]. It continues: "After its establishment, the national Palestinian government will fight for the unity of the countries of confrontation, to complete the liberation of all the Palestinian land . . ." [Section 8]. The Phased Plan in its entirety was broadcast by Saut Falastin Radio, Egypt, on the day of its adoption and may be found reprinted in Netanyahu, *A Place Among the Nations,* pp. 433–34.
2. Yitzhak Zaccai, *Judea, Samaria, and the Gaza District, 1967–1987: Twenty Years of Civil Administration* (Jerusalem: Carta, 1987), p. 14.
3. Dan Polisar, Peace Watch monitoring group.
4. Interview with Yasir Arafat, Radio Monte Carlo, September 1, 1993. Cited in *Jerusalem Post*, December 12, 1993.
5. *Jerusalem Post*, March 22, 1994.
6. Amid Haj Ismail Jabar, *Ha'aretz*, May 15, 1994.
7. *Ha'aretz*, August 10, 1994.
8. Israel Television News, November 10, 1994.
9. *Yediot Aharonot*, November 17, 1994.
10. *Ma'ariv*, November 16, 1994.
11. *Yediot Aharonot*, November 17, 1994.
12. Dan Polisar, Peace Watch monitoring group.
13. *Ma'ariv*, July 22, 1995.
14. *Hatzofeh*, July 13, 1995.
15. *The New York Times*, January 29, 1939.

16. Arafat was quickly caught abusing this exemption. As Prime Minister Rabin put in a report to the Israeli cabinet, "Arafat smuggled into Gaza in his motorcade" several notorious terrorist killers, including Mamdouh Nufal, who organized the 1974 massacre at Maalot of twenty-six schoolchildren; Jihad al Giusi, who took part in planning the 1972 Munich massacre of Israeli athletes; and Mustafa Liftawi, who planned the 1974 massacre on Israel's coastal road, which claimed thirty-five Israeli lives. In this case, Israel's discovery of this flagrant violation of the Oslo accords forced Arafat to turn back these terrorists to Egypt.
17. *Ma'ariv* and *Hatzofeh*, May 14, 1995.
18. Netanyahu, *A Place Among the Nations*, p. 349.
19. *Davar*, July 6, 1995.
20. *Ma'ariv*, July 6, 1995.
21. Rafiq Natshe, member of the Fatah Central Committee, quoted in *Al-Qabas*, December 26, 1989.
22. *Ha'aretz*, August 3, 1995.
23. Arafat and Abu Medien quotes cited in Peace Watch bulletin, August 10, 1995.

CHAPTER VII

1. *Patterns of Global Terrorism, 1994* (Washington: State Department, April 1995), pp. 23–24.
2. See Boaz Ganor, "A New Strategy Against the New Terror," in *PolicyView* (Jerusalem: The Shalem Center, January 19, 1995), pp. 7–10.
3. *Haig v. Agee*, 453 U.S. 280, 307 (1981).